COMBAT AIRCRAFT

125 US NAVY F-4 PHANTOM II UNITS OF THE VIETNAM WAR 1969-73

SERIES EDITOR TONY HOLMES

125

COMBAT AIRCRAFT

Peter E Davies

US NAVY F-4 PHANTOM II UNITS OF THE VIETNAM WAR 1969-73

OSPREY PUBLISHING

OSPREY PUBLISHING
Bloomsbury Publishing Plc
PO Box 883, Oxford, OX1 9PL, UK
1385 Broadway, 5th Floor, New York, NY 10018, USA
E-mail: info@ospreypublishing.com
www.ospreypublishing.com

OSPREY is a trademark of Osprey Publishing Ltd

First published in Great Britain in 2018

A catalogue record for this book is available from the British Library.

ISBN: PB 9781472823601; eBook 9781472823618; ePDF 9781472823595; XML 9781472823588

18 19 20 21 22 10 9 8 7 6 5 4 3 2 1

Edited by Tony Holmes
Cover Artwork by Gareth Hector
Aircraft Profiles by Jim Laurier
Index by Alan Rutter
Originated by PDQ Digital Media Solutions, UK
Printed in China through World Print Ltd.

Osprey Publishing supports the Woodland Trust, the UK's leading woodland conservation charity. Between 2014 and 2018 our donations are being spent on their Centenary Woods project in the UK.

To find out more about our authors and books visit **www.ospreypublishing.com**. Here you will find extracts, author interviews, details of forthcoming events and the option to sign up for our newsletter.

Acknowledgements

The author is grateful to the following individuals for providing memories and photographs for inclusion in this book – Cdr Stephen Barkley US Navy (ret), Lt Bart Bartholomay US Navy (ret), Lt Lynn Batterman US Navy (ret), Lt Cdr Matt Connelly US Navy (ret), Col John Cummings US Marine Corps (ret), Kev Darling, Cdr Curtis R Dosé US Navy (ret), Maj Gen Paul Fratarangelo US Marine Corps (ret), Michael France, Cdr Bill Freckleton US Navy (ret), Capt Brian Grant US Navy (ret), Capt Jerry B Houston US Navy (ret), Cdr Jan Jacobs US Navy (ret), Capt John Nash US Navy (ret), Cdr Stephen Rudloff US Navy (ret), Norm Taylor, Dr István Toperczer and RADM John R Wilson Jr US Navy (ret).

Front Cover

The 197th, and last, MiG kill of the Vietnam War occurred at 1253 hrs on 12 January 1973 when two VF-161 'Chargers' F-4Bs, flying a BARCAP mission from USS *Midway* (CVA-41), intercepted a lone MiG-17. Lt Victor Kovaleski and Lt(jg) Jim Wise in 'Rock River 102' (BuNo 153045), with Lt Pat Arwood and Ens Lynn Oates in a second F-4B, were vectored to intercept a VPAF MiG-17 that had ventured out across the coast to try and down a USAF C-130 Hercules. Flying at around 1000 ft and at 450 knots, the novice MiG pilot, Luu Kim Ngo, of the 923rd Fighter Regiment was picked up sporadically on radar as he flew in a low cloud-base. The two pursuing US Navy crews were quickly able to gain a visual identification on their quarry at a range of four miles and they closed in undetected.

Post-mission, Wise reported that the MiG pilot eventually saw them and used his superior turn rate to roll in behind the F-4s, before turning left and levelling out ahead of them. He then inexplicably turned in the opposite direction, placing himself in Sidewinder acquisition range of the F-4Bs. Kovaleski immediately fired an AIM-9G from 'Rock River 102' and it blew off part of the MiG's tail. Luu Kim Ngo ejected, but his parachute failed to open and his body was later recovered from the sea. Kovaleski fired a second AIM-9G, which turned the MiG into a fireball as it crashed into the sea. Two days later, Kovaleski and Ens D H Plautz were hit by 85 mm AAA while flying a *Blue Tree* reconnaissance escort mission near Than Hoa. With one engine knocked out and the Phantom II suffering a massive fuel leak, Kovaleski and Plautz had little choice but to abandon F-4B BuNo 153068 (previously a MiG killer for Lts 'Bart' Bartholomay and Oran Brown) and await rescue from the sea by an HH-3A helicopter. Their F-4B was the last of 44 aircraft lost by a *Midway* air wing during the war (*Cover artwork by Gareth Hector*)

Previous Spread

VF-142 'Ghostriders' F-4Js perform a four-ship training mission during pre-cruise work-ups in the spring of 1971. The unit would embark in *Enterprise* for the sixth of its seven combat deployments in June of that year. The No 3 jet in this formation, BuNo 155846, became a MiG killer for Lt(jg)s Scott Davis and Geoff Ulrich on 28 December 1972 (during the unit's final Vietnam cruise) and was lost in a non-fatal accident on 3 May 1973 (*US Navy*)

CONTENTS

CHAPTER ONE

THE TIME IN BETWEEN

During their intensive Operation *Rolling Thunder* missions over North Vietnam the US Navy's F-4 Phantom II squadrons on board the aircraft carriers of Task Force 77 (TF 77) had demonstrated the fighter's versatility in an unprecedented variety of tasks. Its initial role as an all-weather fleet defence interceptor had expanded to include successful deployment for ground attack, flak suppression, escort and a range of combat air patrol (CAP) missions. Their duties even included seeing off Soviet Tu-95 'Bear' reconnaissance aircraft that usually overflew US Navy carriers en route to or from the South China Sea. The 1972 Command History for USS *Enterprise* (CVAN-65) records overflights that were escorted by F-4Js 'while in the vicinity of the Task Group. The Soviet crews demonstrated no hostile intent and manoeuvred their aircraft safely and professionally while conducting surveillance of *Enterprise*. The Soviet aircrews were friendly and waved at the escorting F-4 crews, smiling and gesturing to the crews to fly closer so that they could take pictures'.

Over North Vietnam, in contrast, F-4 crews' experiences with Soviet-built aircraft were far from friendly. Thirteen North Vietnamese People's Air Force (VPAF) MiG-17s and MiG-21s, together with two nocturnal An-2 radar calibration aircraft, had been shot down (and a further four enemy aircraft plausibly claimed) by the end of 1968 for the loss of four F-4s to MiGs, despite the frequently disappointing performance of the Phantom II's primary air-to-air missile armament. The 18 squadrons flying F-4B (and a

VF-21's F-4J BuNo 155764/NE 106 is about to take the 'three-wire' for a safe arrestment aboard *Ranger* in 1970 during the carrier's time on *Yankee Station*. Three drop tanks (600-gallon centreline and 370-gallon underwing) were usually only carried for long-range strike or escort missions into Laos or for transit flights. Frequent shortages of the tanks meant that they had to be brought back to the carrier whenever possible. A three-piece folding Corner Reflector for the All Weather Carrier Landing System, with its AN/SPN-42 computer aboard the ship, is extended ahead of the jet's nose-gear door (*US Navy*) few F-4J) Phantom IIs during that period had proven the aircraft's ability to hit ground targets with heavy loads of 250-, 500-, 1000- or 2000-lb bombs, 5-inch Zuni or 2.75-inch free-flight rockets and Mk 20 Rockeye II cluster bombs, among other ordnance, albeit with relatively primitive weapons delivery systems. However, F-4 crews usually considered themselves to be primarily air-to-air fighter pilots for whom ground attack (the job of the VA A-1 Skyraider, A-4 Skyhawk, A-6 Intruder and A-7 Corsair II 'attack' squadrons) was an obligatory diversion from their true role.

North Vietnam was divided into six assigned areas (or Route Packages [RPs]), with the US Navy striking targets in the coastal areas around the port of Haiphong (RP 6B) and RPs 2, 3 and 4, which extended south towards the demilitarised zone (DMZ) between North and South Vietnam. USAF F-4 and F-105 Thunderchief strike formations, flying mainly from Thailand, focused on RPs 5 and 6A to the north and west (including Hanoi) and RP 1, just north of the DMZ. The US Government's constant focus on sortie rates and tonnage of bombs on target as its instruments for measuring perceived success, together with a decline in MiG activity in 1967, meant that US Navy F-4 squadrons were given increasing numbers of attack sorties to perform. Carrying roughly the same bomb-load (typically, six Mk 82 500 lb bombs) as the US Navy's principal bomber in 1965-67, the A-4, F-4Bs could operate from some older carriers like USS *Midway* (CVA-41) and USS *Coral Sea* (CVA-43) with a full complement of air-to-air missiles as well, allowing them to revert to MiGCAP duties if necessary.

President Lyndon Johnson abandoned the three-year-long Operation *Rolling Thunder* offensive on 1 November 1968 in the vain hope that persuasive diplomacy rather than continued bombing of North Vietnam would draw the Hanoi regime into peace negotiations. The last mission of the campaign was flown by F-4Bs of VF-142 and VF-143 from Carrier Air Wing (CVW) 14, embarked in USS *Constellation* (CVA-64). The sustained USAF and US Navy attacks of *Rolling Thunder*, which some observers in Hanoi later judged to have severely weakened North Vietnam's military strength, were ended and aerial activity was restricted to territory south of the 20th parallel. However, the campaign had been a costly one for the US Navy, with 377 aircrew killed in action and around 116 taken prisoner between 1965 and 1968. It had lost 601 aircraft during that time, with 1000 more damaged.

The bombing pause gave North Vietnam ample opportunity to repair the damage it had suffered from more than 640,000 tons of bombs. The communists could strengthen their defences and increase the movement of military supplies into Laos, Cambodia and South Vietnam. MiG airfields

A red-shirted armourer attaches impact fuses to Zuni rockets housed in LAU-10 pods that have been uploaded onto an F-4. The five-inch Zuni unguided rocket reached speeds exceeding Mach 3, and continued to leave a fiery trail throughout most of its flightpath towards the target. Its effect on AAA emplacements could be devastating, as the weapon had the capability to be fused to explode ten feet above the ground, spreading shrapnel widely (*US Navy*)

were also refurbished, increased in number and re-stocked with fighters from the USSR and China to supplement more than 50 that had been sheltered at bases in the latter country. The numbers of SA-2 'Guideline' surface-to-air missile (SAM) and radar-guided anti-aircraft artillery (AAA) sites were also greatly increased.

For the F-4 units, many of their routine activities after March 1968, when bombing was restricted to targets below the 20th parallel, continued as before.

Barrier combat air patrol (BARCAP) flights were on alert in case of VPAF attempts to attack US Navy warships patrolling off the coast of North Vietnam. Reconnaissance flights over enemy territory by RA-5C Vigilante, RF-8A Crusader and EA-3B Skywarrior aircraft continued, requiring fighter escort by F-4s. They also joined US Marine Corps Phantom II crews in protecting radar reconnaissance aircraft during their offshore orbits. Strike operations continued in the permitted areas below the 20th parallel and in Laos and South Vietnam. Weather was often the primary hindrance, but the attempts to intercept supply convoys moving south were sometimes well rewarded. Repeated attacks on roads, bridges and fuel depots appeared to reduce the number of convoys, although the drivers also became more adept at disguising their presence.

F-4J BuNo 155872/NK 113 from VF-143 (which has adorned its jets with *BEST IN THE WEST* titling beneath the Battle E – the US Navy's 'top performance award presented to the aviation squadron in each competitive category that achieves the highest standards of performance readiness and efficiency') flies 'shotgun' for an RA-5C of RVAH-7 'Peacemakers of the Fleet' in 1970. Despite being valued at $14m ($90m in today's money), the Vigilante's only self-defence was its high speed as a clean, powerful reconnaissance platform. Its limited cockpit visibility made an F-4 escort a necessity as a second set of eyes and as a MiG deterrent. However, in many cases, the Phantom II could be just as vulnerable to enemy defences as the RA-5C (*US Navy*)

FINER PHANTOM IIs

Although the nature of the missions was substantially unchanged, the introduction of the revised F-4J brought some improvements to the Phantom II units' capabilities from 1967. Its Westinghouse AN/AWG-10 pulse-Doppler fire control system and AN/APG-59 multi-mode radar enabled more effective aerial target acquisition, particularly at medium and low altitudes, where its 'look down' capability allowed it to locate, search and track targets that would have otherwise disappeared into ground-effect clutter on the F-4B's AN/APG-72 radar picture. The original 32-inch meshed radar dish was initially retained, but it was eventually replaced by a more robust fibreglass version in late-production F-4Js. On all but the first batches of J-models (which had 'clean' radomes), a small ALQ-51A/100 DECM fairing beneath the radome replaced the F-4B's elongated 'chin' pod.

The F-4J's improved AN/AJB-7 bombing system with an AN/ASQ-91 weapons release computer gave more accurate bombing results than the nuclear-optimised AN/AJB-3A loft-toss system in the F-4B. AN/AJB-7 could also guide the AGM-12C Bullpup B air-to-ground missile, although that option was seldom used. The system's ground-mapping mode was useful, but ground attack in the F-4J still relied very much on the aiming skills of the aircrew when compared with the more advanced automated

VF-213 F-4B BuNo 153017 from *Kitty Hawk* flies escort for a VAW-114 E-2A Hawkeye AEW aircraft – which made its first deployment in 1965 embarked in that very carrier – during CVW-11's 1967-68 Vietnam cruise. CVA-63 was also the first 'flattop' to boast the complex Naval Tactical Data System that linked the E-2A to both the carrier and the airborne strike force, providing sophisticated early warning and airborne control facilities. However, the system took some time to achieve full operational effectiveness. VF-213 made six wartime cruises with CVW-11 on board *Kitty Hawk* (US Navy)

systems in the A-6A Intruder and A-7 Corsair II dedicated attack aircraft. The average visual bombing CEP (circular error of probability) for the F-4 was 483 ft, compared with 111 ft for an A-7.

Initially, poor reliability hampered the combat introduction of the complex AN/AWG-10. However, better training and the gradual replacement of delicate vacuum tube components with solid-state circuit boards reduced 'down time'. VMFA-333 Radar Intercept Officer (RIO) Capt John Cummings was a vital figure in honing the new radar on board USS *America* (CVA-66) in 1972;

'We had some problems at first because the AWG-10 pushed the limits of electronic engineering in those days. Some company techs were with us on board *America*, and between them and our own radar techs we were able to make the system work. I did lose a shot at a MiG on 10 September because my damn radar quit, but these things happen.'

F-4Js also had the AN/ASW-25A data link system, trialled in the small number of F-4Gs (converted B-models) flown in combat by VF-213 from USS *Kitty Hawk* (CVA-63) in 1965-66. The system was intended to pass voiceless data from the carrier or E-2A Hawkeye airborne early warning (AEW) aircraft for controlling the Phantom II via its autopilot, including 'hands off' automatic carrier landings (ACLS). The F-4J's approach power compensator system, popularly known as 'auto-throttles', and its flying controls operated without pilot input for a hands-off landing, which some pilots admitted could be better than they could achieve themselves. For carrier landings at night, considerable faith in the technology was required. This sophisticated system was not sufficiently developed during the war years to be effective as an airborne controller in combat, however, although ACLS was used. Lt Michael Riggio made the first ACLS Mode 1 automatic landing on board *Kitty Hawk* in his VF-213 F-4J on 16 September 1970.

A pair of powerful General Electric J79-GE-17 turbojet engines developing a total of 35,800 lb of thrust compensated for the F-4J's empty weight increase of 2881 lb over the F-4B, despite a 231-gallon reduction in internal fuel to accommodate the larger AN/AWG-10. The slotted leading edges of the horizontal stabilisers, combined with locked inboard leading-edge flaps and a 16.5-degree 'droop' in the ailerons for take-off and landing, reduced approach speed by 12 knots and improved rotation for catapult launching. An increased sink rate on landing because of the F-4J's weight gain required the installation of a stronger main undercarriage and wider tyres, with the latter having to be accommodated in deeper wheel-wells. The new tyres reduced the number of blow-outs experienced by Phantom II crews on landing, although they could aquaplane, unlike the narrower F-4B tyres, when landing on wet runways.

There was also some reduction in the J79s' characteristic smoke trail that made the F-4B, at 'cruise' throttle settings, visible to enemy pilots at distances exceeding 15 miles. MiGs left inconspicuous smoke trails and their smaller radar signature made them harder to detect. Research into reduced J79 emissions and, in particular, combustion systems and the hydrogen content of JP-4 and JP-8 jet fuels continued throughout the 1970s, but in combat pilots usually had to resort to the standard, but fuel-wasting, practice of using minimum afterburner to try and eliminate their tell-tale smoke signature. As F-4B RIO Lt Cdr J B Souder put it, 'the aeroplane smoked like a coal stove. Our big, black smoke trail was a deadly tip-off to an adversary'. For the last few MiG engagements of the war, particularly the 28 December 1972 MiG-21 kill by Lt(jg)s Scott Davis and Geoffrey Ulrich of VF-142, an anti-smoke chemical additive was used in the engines of their F-4J (BuNo 155846).

J-models equipped four TF 77 squadrons (VF-21, VF-33, VF-102 and VF-154) by the end of 1968, and by 1972 11 of the US Navy squadrons and one US Marine Corps carrier-borne unit (VMFA-333) operating in the Gulf of Tonkin had F-4Js, with four still flying F-4Bs.

The VF-213 crew of F-4J BuNo 157265/ NH 111, armed with ten Mk 82 bombs and two AIM-9Gs, prepare for a strike mission from *Kitty Hawk* in 1970. The carrier spent 138 days on line during this, its fifth combat cruise. The 'Black Lions' had moved to NAS Miramar from NAS Moffett Field, California, in 1961, remaining there for 36 years and converting from the F-3B Demon to the Phantom II in 1964. Over the next 12 years VF-213 would fly F-4Bs, F-4Gs and finally F-4Js, after which it transitioned to the F-14A (*US Navy*)

AIR-TO-AIR

Although MiG encounters were rare, the psychological impact a positive engagement with a VPAF fighter had on a pilot was considerable. As Capt Jerry 'Devil' Houston recalled, 'MiGs were funny – you ran into them or you didn't. Many great fighter pilots never saw one. But ask a fighter pilot what he'd give to get a kill, and you might get embarrassed. RIOs felt the same'. The experience of those who had fought MiGs was valuable, but many Naval Aviators left the service after *Rolling Thunder*. This meant that when the carrier force was once again called into action for Operation *Linebacker* in 1972 numerous crews had no previous combat experience. Low re-enlistment rates for first-tour sailors also reduced efficiency and morale aboard some carriers. Often, aircrew entered battle without receiving the benefit of the hard-won knowledge of departing aircrew who had flown in *Rolling Thunder* but then sought more lucrative employment with airlines.

An increasing concern as *Rolling Thunder* ended was the F-4's relatively disappointing success rate (in all three services) against the far less sophisticated MiG-17 'Fresco-A/C' and MiG-21 'Fishbed' throughout

Loaded with six LAU-10 Zuni pods and two AIM-9G Sidewinders on its LAU-17 inboard pylons, F-4J BuNo 155540/AE 112 prepares to launch from *America* on a flak suppression mission with bombed-up BuNo 155552/AE 110, also from VF-102. The squadron made a single wartime deployment, joining VF-33 to make the F-4J's combat debut on a cruise that saw the unit return to NAS Oceana, Virginia, by mid-December 1968. Two VF-102 jets were lost during the cruise, one of which was AE 112. It crashed into the Gulf of Tonkin on 25 July 1968 after being damaged by AAA (or possibly the premature detonation of one of its bombs) whilst attacking the railway marshalling yard at Vinh. Pilot Lt Charles Parish was killed and Lt Robert Fant captured (*US Navy*)

the campaign. The VPAF's air-to-air successes as a proportion of all US losses increased from three per cent in 1966 to 22 per cent in the first three months of 1968. After the first MiG kill by an F-4J on 10 July 1968, there were no further confirmed successes for Phantom II units for 21 months.

The reduction in carrier operations in 1968-69 took the F-4s out of most of the action over North Vietnam and confined them to bombing missions against transport and supply targets south of the 20th parallel. Ironically, the smaller carriers such as USS *Bon Homme Richard* (CVA-31) and USS *Intrepid* (CVS-11), with F-8 Crusaders embarked, were left on the line and scored five MiG kills in 1968 as a result. The costly sophistication of the F-4's weapons system had encouraged the belief that kill-to-loss rates against MiGs should have exceeded the ten-to-one ratio claimed by US pilots during the Korean War. Statistics could be used to show that the simpler F-8, armed with cannon and Sidewinders, had the best success rate against MiGs if a 'kills per engagement' figure was used. There were certainly many rumours that MiG pilots preferred to fight F-4s, and avoided the Crusaders. In at least one May 1972 engagement a MiG-17 pilot ejected when he realised that VF-211 F-8J pilot Lt Jerry Tucker had a good Sidewinder-firing position on him. The US Navy officially denied Tucker credit for this success – the Crusader's last aerial victory.

Despite isolated incidents such as the Tucker manoeuvring kill, the VPAF was often very effective in the skies over North Vietnam, particularly after the introduction of MiG-21s in November 1965. With the advantage of Soviet-constructed ground control systems, integrated with ground-to-air gun and missile emplacements, the MiG pilots could operate close to their bases in the relatively small area of North Vietnam in which the majority of the US Navy's targets were located. MiG-21s were used mainly against the larger USAF strike packages entering North Vietnam from Thailand, where there was a lack of adequate long-range radar coverage to warn of intercepting MiGs. The 'Fishbed' pilots set up ambush positions at high altitude, swooping in behind the attackers at supersonic speed to launch their missiles and then dive away for home before the F-4 escorts could catch them (see *Osprey Aircraft of the Aces 135 – MiG-21 Aces of the Vietnam War* for further details). The US Navy's excellent offshore radar coverage ruled out these tactics against Alpha strikes entering from the Gulf of Tonkin, which were usually opposed by MiG-17s instead (see *Osprey Aircraft of the Aces 130 – MiG-17/19 Aces of the Vietnam War* for further details).

Successive interruptions of the bombing campaign allowed the VPAF to establish 13 jet-capable airfields by 1972, many of them in forward locations in southern North Vietnam for

temporary staging use. The limited endurance of its fighters was sufficient for them to deal with the US Navy strike 'packages' that usually appeared twice daily, and their agility usually enabled them to out-manoeuvre the heavier US fighters, which were not designed for close-in air-to-air fighting.

Have Drill pilot and future MiG killer Lt Cdr Ronald 'Mugs' McKeown, who tested a captured MiG-17, famously described fighting a 'Fresco' with a Phantom II as being like 'a knife-fight in a phone booth'. He identified the secret of success as staying out of range of the MiG's guns and using the F-4's superior speed and rate of roll to perform a series of barrel rolls that would eventually allow it to turn back and attack the VPAF fighter. A MiG-17 had about half the wing loading of an F-4B and weighed 75 per cent less. Its gun armament could be very destructive at close range, where Phantom II crews were unable to utilise their sophisticated long-range, radar-controlled AIM-7 Sparrow missiles.

F-4 crews also complained that, unlike the MiG pilots, their frequent lack of precise airborne or ship-borne early warning of enemy fighters made them vulnerable to surprise attack, particularly when MiGs were vectored onto them from low altitude or behind, making them harder to see. Also, F-4s tasked with escorting strike or reconnaissance missions were supposed to stay with their charges, rather than heading off to pursue enemy fighters. Crews on MiGCAP missions had rather more flexibility in that situation, although in 1971 and early 1972 MiGs generally avoided US Navy fighters, and never ventured close enough to be chased.

MISSILES AND 'HIT-ILES'

The AIM-7 Sparrow originated as an effective beyond-visual-range missile, but over North Vietnam pilots were hardly ever able to use it in that way in case they hit unexpected friendly aircraft. The requirement to obtain

Flying closer formation than on an Alpha strike, but still representing the core of a strike package, this assembly of naval air power includes squadrons from *Kitty Hawk*'s CVW-11 during their 1973-74 Vietnam cruise. The two Phantom II flights are from VF-213 (centre, including an unmarked F-4J) and VF-114, while the strike element is made up of A-7Es from VA-192 (lower, rear) and VA-195 (top), led by four A-6A Intruders from VA-52. Intruders were scheduled for early catapult launches as their large, draggy external ordnance loads increased fuel consumption. The codename 'Alpha strike' indicted an attack on a top priority target (*US Navy*) a visual identification of a potential target aircraft usually meant that it was inside the minimum 'homing' range for an AIM-7 before it could be positively identified. At that range a gun, which had been designed out of the F-4 at an early stage in its evolution, might have been a viable alternative, although many Phantom II pilots felt that their fighter lacked the manoeuvrability at lower speeds to use such a weapon effectively. Instead, the AIM-9 Sidewinder usually became the only viable weapon.

MiG pilots, many of whom remained in action throughout the war rather than serving for fixed tours of duty lasting about eight to ten months as their US Navy counterparts did, rapidly gained experience during the course of *Rolling Thunder*, and they were able to develop tactics that made the best use of their fighters. On 19 November 1967 both F-4Bs in a VF-151 TARCAP (target combat air patrol) were shot down, with two crew killed and two captured, by a carefully coordinated pack of six MiG-17s and MiG-21s operating from a forward airfield at Kien An. US Navy F-4 crews claimed only one MiG between 30 October 1967 and 9 May 1968, that kill being credited to a VF-96 'Fighting Falcons' jet two days after the unit had lost a Phantom II to an 'Atoll' missile fired from a MiG-21. The F-4B's radar had failed during a confused dogfight with several 'Fishbeds', leaving its crew blind to the enemy missile.

The US Navy's 1968 kill-to-loss ratio remained at two MiGs for two F-4s, although 27 air-to-air missiles had been fired by Phantom II crews. Reports of missile unreliability, near-miss blue-on-blue incidents and difficulty in tackling MiGs at close quarters increased throughout 1968, and several engagements had involved F-4 crews firing almost their full complements of weapons without hits. For example, on 25 August 1968 VF-143 F-4B crews escorting an Alpha strike fired three AIM-7s and seven AIM-9s at three MiG-21s, but they all failed to reach their targets. Comprehensive remedial action was clearly needed.

An F-4J with a typical CAP load of two AIM-7E-2 Sparrows, four AIM-9G Sidewinders and a centreline 600-gallon drop tank. Triple ejector racks (TERs) are attached beneath the inboard pylons, as ground attack ordnance was also carried on many missions, and the outboard pylons – also empty on this occasion – were usually kept in place to save man-hours aboard ship. ECM antennas are visible beneath the air inlets and ahead of the wing control surfaces. This particular aircraft (BuNo 155800/NG 100) achieved fame as a triple MiG killer with VF-96 on 10 May 1972 (*US Navy*)

Significant improvements to the missile armament were years away, with the post-war development of the all-aspect AIM-9L Sidewinder using a more powerful warhead and better fusing, together with the far more reliable AIM-7F Sparrow. Little could be done to make the F-4B/J a more effective 'dogfighter', although leading-edge wing slats (to improve turn performance) were added to the refurbished F-4Js in the F-4S upgrade programme from 1977. Stalling during tight turns could occur even with experienced pilots in control. Lt Cdr 'Mugs' McKeown's victory over a MiG-17 on 23 May 1972 included a few moments when his VF-161 F-4B (BuNo 153020) was tumbling out of control as he made a hard, nose-high turn to get behind the VPAF fighter. He recovered by using a full forward push on the control column until the jet rolled 'wings level', albeit inverted. Generally, the main chances of better performance would come from improved tactics and better maintenance and reliability for the radar and missiles.

Formal investigation of the problems began in May 1968 when Capt Frank 'Whip' Ault was commissioned to produce a report based on recommendations concerning air-to-air missile performance that he had made the previous year while captain of *Coral Sea*. The carrier had lost no fewer than 52 aircraft in combat during its first three cruises, three of them to MiGs, with only one MiG shoot-down by its fighter squadrons in return. Ault had strong views on the conduct of naval air warfare, and his subsequent report (titled the *Air-to-Air Missile Capability Review*) released in early 1969 was far-reaching into naval procedures, industrial standards of production and missile maintenance.

He found inadequacies in the level of quality that the US Navy expected from its suppliers, and a reliance on performance statistics provided by manufacturers that were based on unrealistic, ideal test conditions, rather than actual combat situations. These figures suggested success rates of up to 90 per cent, with more exacting re-tests in 1965 still showing at least 50 per cent 'hit' rates. The *Rolling Thunder* success rate had actually been around eight per cent for the AIM-7 and 15 per cent for the AIM-9. Ault's report identified poor standards of missile testing, maintenance and storage, and a tendency to leave weapons aboard F-4s for several consecutive missions so that the rigours of carrier launches and landings disturbed their delicate electronic components. This was particularly true of the AIM-7, where a shortage of trained missile technicians on board TF 77 carriers further reduced serviceability. As MiG killer Jerry Houston, who converted to the F-4 from the F-8 in 1971, commented;

'We believed in the Sidewinder. The radars weren't reliable and we feared that their [search] strobes would give us away and cost us a shot in a MiG engagement. Only our radar systems' poor supply support kept us from having equal success with the radar/Sparrow system – that is, having Sparrows that would work. The missile of choice was always the Sidewinder. We would fly into a kill position for the Sidewinder, and once you did that a kill was practically assured. The RIOs, indignant at first, came to see our point of view, especially given the MiG kills.'

One of Ault's investigative teams also drew attention to the lack of effective air-to-air training and the widespread use of F-4s for ground attack missions as reasons for the disappointing aerial combat performance.

Capt Frank Ault was chosen by Vice Admiral Tom Connolly, Deputy Chief of Naval Operations (Air), to present a report on the shortcomings of US Navy air-to-air combat in the early stages of the Vietnam War. His observations on the subject while he was captain of *Coral Sea* for two combat tours, combined with his outspoken nature, made him an ideal choice to bring basic changes to the ways in which the naval air war was conducted. His investigations revealed shortcomings from the weapons manufacturing stage through to the training of air- and groundcrew and the use of missile systems in combat (*US Navy*)

An AIM-7 accelerates ahead of a VF-21 F-4J host. The missile was originally intended for firing at large, non-manoeuvring targets at a range of about 12 miles. Launching the missile required a coordinated switch-setting and radar monitoring procedure by pilot and RIO. A full-systems radar lock-on required five seconds for the missile to be correctly programmed, with allowances for performance variations due to altitude and temperature. If the target manoeuvred beyond 3g the lock would usually be broken and the missile 'went ballistic'. Many early misfired launches were caused by a failure in the wafer-switch that made the contact between the missile and the aircraft. Replacement of the switch every time the missile was downloaded was the best cure. Sparrows were occasionally expended against unusual targets, including a North Vietnamese patrol boat which had set out to try and capture the crew of an RVAH-7 Vigilante that was shot down offshore from Than Hoa (*US Navy*)

Pilots had usually flown a few air-to-air sorties in training, typically against other F-4s, rather than dissimilar aircraft that would have been better simulators of MiG tactics.

In combat, crews often overestimated the tracking ability of their missiles, launching them outside their design parameters of distance and angle from the target, or at a manoeuvring fighter. Neither the AIM-7 nor the more basic AIM-9 had been designed for use against the highly manoeuvrable targets that F-4s met regularly over North Vietnam. The AIM-7 was intended for long-range fleet defence interception from the forward quarter or side-on against bomber targets approaching the carrier on a straight-and-level course at medium or high altitudes. At lower altitudes, the weapon could easily lose its radar lock-in ground effect.

After launching an AIM-7, the F-4's RIO had to keep the target illuminated ('strobing') by his radar and the pilot had to fly a steady course without manoeuvring for fear of breaking the missile's radar lock so that it ran wild. The missile originally had to impact its target in order to explode, although a more practical proximity fuse was installed in the 1959 AIM-7D and subsequent versions. In daylight, the crew of the targeted aircraft might see the copious white smoke trail from the missile, but they would have little time to attempt avoiding action.

If the Sparrows (usually fired in pairs) failed to destroy the intruder in a head-on interception, the F-4 pilot could make a 180-degree turn to use his secondary AIM-9 Sidewinder armament for a stern attack from immediately behind the target. These combat conditions hardly ever occurred in Vietnam after the first few encounters in June 1965, however, putting F-4 crews at a severe disadvantage. In practice, the nitrogen-cooled AIM-9D, while generally reliable, could sometimes disintegrate soon after launching or become diverted by random heat sources such as the sun, clouds, the ground or a 'friendly' aircraft. It did have the advantages of a longer, 11-mile range and a double-sized warhead compared with the early AIM-9B used in 1965-66.

Preparing to launch an AIM-7 or AIM-9 required a complex series of switch-setting operations and radar manipulation by the crew, who had to look down into the cockpit to perform these procedures rather than watching the target. Again, this process was quite impractical during a swirling aerial dogfight against agile enemy fighters. The RIO, as a second pair of eyes, could be crucial when the cockpit workload was heavy, but his duties could extend far beyond operating the radar system. John Cummings was an important developer of F-4 back-seat procedures;

'With some aviators, you were a full-time systems operator, handling the radar, ECM gear, etc. A few pilots required a little more help, and your duties expanded to whatever needed to be done. On daylight missions in high threat areas, most of our attention was focused outside the aircraft looking for flak, SAMs, MiGs and the target.'

As former VF-111 RIO Bill 'Farkle' Freckleton recalled;

'Fleet defence interception was not relevant to the situation in Vietnam, other than that it laid the basic groundwork for systems familiarity and crew coordination. The actual systematic procedures for a "150 to 180 degrees to go" interception, with conversion on a straight-and-level "bogie" [intruder target] were not applicable. The greater preponderance of RAG [Replacement Air Group] training in the F-4B and F-4J at VF-121 "Pacemakers" was fleet defensive. A very few (less than six) hops were dedicated to actual ACM [air combat manoeuvring], and even then one or two were sometimes waived to get guys into the fleet.'

Freckleton also commented on the unreliability of the F-4B radar;

'We used hand signals a lot in Vietnam to communicate between aircraft, and one of the most used signals was the left-to-right sweeping motion of the hand [indicating a sweep by the radar antenna], followed by a thumbs down or thumbs up, or a rocking motion of the hand to indicate whether the radar was up, down or "shaky" (degraded).'

As a strike formation neared the coast to go 'feet dry', F-4B RIOs used their radar in 'mapping' mode to check topographical features along the coast, before switching to 'search and track'. Bill Freckleton explained;

'Once we were about 20 miles from the beach we concentrated on the air search, operating the search radar in a scan pattern that ensured the best possible radar coverage in the direction of the potential airborne threat. We hardly used the system for radar navigation or targeting, but used it extensively in the search and track modes.'

USAF F-4 crews tended to try and compensate for their temperamental radars and the missiles' unpredictable performance by firing all the weapons of one type (AIM-7 or AIM-9) in a single salvo in the hope of increasing their chances of a kill. US Navy crews tended to be more precise, generally firing one missile at a time, thereby increasing the number of potential firing passes. Carrier launch weight limits often meant that only the rear pair of AIM-7s were uploaded, which also resulted in more selective missile firing.

Ault's recommendation for improved missiles was answered to some extent by the introduction of the longer-ranged AIM-7E-2, dubbed (slightly optimistically) the 'Dogfight' Sparrow. Initially available in 1968 in small numbers, it was more manoeuvrable and, thanks to an additional internal electronic plug, could be launched at a shorter minimum range (1500 ft rather than 3000 ft) than the standard AIM-7E, 25,000 of which had been manufactured. The weapon's proximity fusing was also improved, but there were numerous cases of premature detonation just ahead of the aircraft, tracking anomalies or failure of the rocket motor to light up, although it could be launched from a turning F-4.

A time-honoured dive-bombing delivery by VF-111 'Sundowners' F-4B BuNo 150466/NL 204 in 1972 is a reminder that the US Navy never adopted laser-guided weapons on anything but a trial basis during the Vietnam War, relying on World War 2 delivery techniques and very simple bomb-aiming devices for its fighter-bombers (*US Navy*)

Armament 'ordies' used a crude 'hernia bar' inserted into the fuse receptacle of a Mk 82 bomb to lift it into position on an F-4's TER in what was clearly a labour-intensive process that was very often repeated three times a day. Lack of space on deck meant moving ordnance around in manually operated carts, rather than by motorised MJ-1 loaders available to USAF crews ashore, and uploading bombs with sheer muscle power. Youth, energy and the ability to work repeated 14-hour shifts amidst extreme noise, danger and uncertain weather were prerequisites for the job. During periods of particularly intense action on some carriers, time might allow only one meal a day, with only salt water to wash in and drinking water that tasted of jet fuel (*US Navy*)

The 'Dogfight' Sparrow duly became the standard AIM-7 version from 1971, and its overall success rate in combat of 12 per cent was at least a three per cent improvement on the AIM-7E, even though reliability was still lacking. Out of 281 AIM-7E-2s fired by US Navy and USAF F-4s, only 34 kills resulted. It was responsible for just one US Navy F-4 kill – a MiG-21 credited to Lt Cdr Robert Tucker and Lt(jg) Bruce Edens of VF-103 on 10 August 1972, although a second 'Fishbed' was destroyed by a USAF 432nd TRW F-4E flown by exchange pilots Capt Lawrence Richard (US Marine Corps) and Lt Cdr Mike Ettel (US Navy) 48 hours later. The remaining 24 US Navy and US Marines Corps F-4 kills between 19 January 1972 and 1 January 1973 were scored with AIM-9Gs (50 of which were fired), whereas from April 1965 to March 1970 half of the 14 MiGs shot down by Phantom IIs had fallen to AIM-7s.

The AIM-9G variant of the Sidewinder became available to the US Navy after *Rolling Thunder*. Superior to the USAF's standard AIM-9E, which could not be launched accurately with the F-4 turning at more than 2g, the AIM-9G could be released in a high-g turn. In due course it had the advantage of Sidewinder Extended Acquisition Mode (SEAM), which slaved the missile's seeker head to the aircraft's radar or to a pilot's helmet-mounted sight. It proved to be more reliable than the USAF's AIM-9J version, used during the 1972 *Linebacker* operations, and achieved a 42 per cent success rate during the frantic MiG engagements of 10 May 1972, including a record 'three AIM-9s for three MiGs destroyed' performance by Lt Randy Cunningham and Lt(jg) Willie Driscoll of VF-96.

A further US Navy development, the AIM-9H became available in the final months of the war. It was the first solid-state Sidewinder with consequent improvements in reliability and robustness and improved tracking of manoeuvring targets. Its fins were driven by more powerful actuators, enabling it to turn more tightly. Although it was available in small numbers, the missile had a far more successful kill ratio than any previous AIM-9 model, and it acquitted itself well at lower altitudes.

Well over half of all MiG losses occurred below 7000 ft altitude, whereas the MiGs were more successful above 15,000 ft, where the AIM-7 system was meant to be at its most efficient. In effect, the AIM-9 became the Phantom II squadrons' weapon of choice when aerial combat resumed in 1972, while the USAF, operating more frequently at higher altitudes where radar-guided missiles worked more efficiently, continued to prioritise the AIM-7.

Sidewinders were usually fired from the 'lag pursuit' position, where a Phantom II pilot tried to get behind a MiG's 'six o'clock' and draw back far enough to give the missile the correct range for it to track the target. As MiG-19 killer Lt 'Bart' Bartholomay explained;

'The MiG-17, MiG-19 and MiG-21 all had approximately the same wingspan. Our [F-4B] gunsight had two circles which, although not specifically designed for it, helped the pilot judge the distance to a MiG. If the wingspan extended across the outer circle, you were approximately 600 ft behind (the minimum range of the AIM-9D at the time), and if it extended across the inner circle, you were approximately two miles behind (approaching the missile's maximum range).'

Have Doughnut was the codename for the testing of the Soviet-built MiG-21F-13 that became available after its Iraqi air force pilot, Capt Monir Radfa, defected with it to Israel on 16 August 1966. After 100 hours of flight-testing by the Israeli Defense Force Air Force, the aeroplane was loaned to the USAF in January 1968 for three months as part of a deal involving the sale of F-4Es to Israel. Air Force Systems Command managed the tests at Groom Lake, which, like the later MiG-17 programme, yielded invaluable information for USAF and US Navy aircrew and de-mystified many earlier suppositions about the Soviet fighters (*DoD*)

HAVE KNOWLEDGE

A better understanding of the strengths and drawbacks of the enemy fighters would be key factors in improving the performance of F-4 crews in 1972, and this was made possible through a secret project that had begun at Groom Lake, Nevada, some four years earlier. The USAF negotiated the loan of a MiG-21F-13 from Israel as part of a deal to supply F-4Es to the Israeli Defense Force Air Force. The fighter, appropriated by Israel when its Iraqi pilot defected in August 1966, flew 102 sorties (25 of which were made by US Navy pilot Cdr Tom Cassidy) during the course of 1968 prior to being returned to Israel.

The tests, labelled *Have Doughnut* (Air Force Flight Test Center test programmes were identified by a '*Have*' code), analysed structural and performance features of the MiG-21. Areas where the aircraft was inferior to its American counterparts included its lack of nose-wheel steering, poor visibility from the cockpit and unreliable compressed-air-powered wheel brakes. Pilots were impressed with its small size, low radar signature and Mach 2 speed, all of which combined to make the lightweight fighter a formidable opponent. The MiG-21 was found to be comparable in many ways to the F-8 Crusader at around 15,000 ft, although it was more manoeuvrable at very low speeds despite heavy 'stick' forces that required strenuous use of its long control column. Compared with the F-4, the 'Fishbed' had crude weapons systems and an unstable gunsight. Like the Phantom II, the MiG-21 rapidly lost energy in a steep turn at speeds below 400 knots. It also displayed inadequate acceleration when compared with the F-4 and suffered from severe buffeting at low altitudes and high speed.

Later in 1968 the characteristics of the MiG-17 'Fresco' were also explored, again thanks to Israel, which loaned two MiG-17Fs that had inadvertently landed at an Israeli airfield on 12 August 1968. The first Polish-built aircraft began tests, coded *Have Drill*, in January 1969 with US Navy participation, initially via a visit by Korean War veteran Cdr 'Doc' Townsend from VF-121, who wanted real fighter tactics re-instated in the F-4 community, and was impressed by what was happening at Groom

Lake. He had set up a small ACM training programme in VF-121 in 1967, and recommended that other US Navy pilots should experience *Have Drill/Have Doughnut* comparative flights. In due course, a cadre, supervised by Cdr Foster 'Tooter' Teague and including Lt Cdrs Jerry 'Devil' Houston, Ron 'Mugs' McKeown, Mike Welch and others from VF-121 and VF-124, began work in 1969. By then Townsend had become executive officer of VF-143, where he continued spreading his doctrine of more adventurous ACM tactics, prior to returning to command VF-121.

The second MiG-17F, used mainly as a spare, commenced flying in March for *Have Ferry*. Tests continued until June 1969, with a focus on developing tactics that would take advantage of the Soviet fighters' weaknesses, which included a strong tendency to enter an uncontrollable roll to the left at 570 knots and a tendency for the flying controls to become virtually inoperable at around 520 knots when at low altitude. American pilots judged the 'Fresco' to be a crude, simple, strong aircraft with very poor visibility from the cockpit. However, as Topgun instructor John Nash, who flew the MiGs, commented, 'That airplane, at 300 knots, could do a 6g, 360-degree turn and not lose more than five knots, whereas the Phantom II would have done that and been down to landing speed'. The 'Fresco' was flown against F-4s, F-8s and other US Navy types in more than 200 sorties.

In 1972 US Navy pilots would encounter MiG-17s rather than MiG-21s in almost half of their aerial engagements, while USAF crews were more likely to meet MiG-21s or MiG-19s. Data from all three programmes (together with test results from a Cambodian MiG-17F that was tested at Phu Cat air base in South Vietnam in *Have Privilege*) was then passed on to the USAF Fighter Weapons School and to the newly formed Naval Fighter Weapons School (NFWS), better known as Topgun.

Have Doughnut pilots formulated new tactics for use against the MiG-21, these emphasising an aggressive approach where F-4 pilots kept their speed above 450 knots and disengaged if the fight became slow, only re-engaging if they had a speed advantage and the chance to use missiles. Whenever possible, vertical manoeuvres were recommended, particularly against the MiG-17. *Have Drill* showed that an F-4 pilot could easily out-run the MiG-17, allowing his wingman to fall in behind the enemy jet and launch a missile. It was considered essential to stay out of range of the MiG's guns.

This ex-Syrian air force MiG-17F 'Fresco-C' was loaned to the USAF by Israel in Project *Have Drill* after two such examples accidentally landed at Beset airfield in northern Israel on 12 August 1968 when their pilots became lost during a navigation exercise. This aircraft was used for the majority of the secret evaluation sorties at Groom Lake from January 1969, with the resulting data being passed to Topgun instructors via the US Navy's lead pilot in the tests, Cdr 'Tooter' Teague. The second MiG-17F, known as *Have Ferry* and used as a spare, also retained its Syrian air force camouflage, with US insignia and identitfication stripes added by the Israelis. The jet was eventually lost on 23 August 1979 when it entered an uncontrollable spin during an engagement with a US Navy F-5. Pilot Lt Cdr Hugh 'Bandit' Brown was killed in the resulting crash (*DoD*)

The reports from the programme endorsed the US Navy's 'loose deuce' combat formation, which consisted of two mutually supporting F-4s. It was seen to be far more effective than the USAF's 'fluid four' formation in which two wingmen spent most of their time trying to keep formation with their flight leader, who was the 'shooter' if a fight occurred. RIOs were trained to combine a visual watch on the aft 180 degrees portion of the field of vision with operation of the radar, while the pilot concentrated his attention on the forward quarter.

The various *Have* test programmes formed the basis of the US Navy's much-improved record in air-to-air combat during the 1972 *Linebacker* operations, and they became textbook material for the emerging Topgun syllabus. Indeed, some training sorties were flown by NFWS personnel during the final months of *Have Drill*.

TOP MISSILE

Capt 'Whip' Ault's insistence that better air-to-air training was an urgent, primary requirement coincided with the realisation by many pilots, particularly those from the F-8 Crusader community, that air-to-air skills had been lost with the closure of the US Navy's Fleet Air Gunnery Unit in 1960 and the new emphasis on missiles-only armament. Pressure to reinstate those skills pre-dated the Ault Report, and in 1966 VX-4 (an air development squadron), carried out *Project Plan*, flying F-4Bs against a variety of other fighters including the F-104 and F-8 as MiG-21 simulators. The outcome was a boost for the Phantom II as an air-to-air fighter as long as it maintained high speed (570-600 knots) in a fight and manoeuvred well in the vertical plane.

Ault's initiative incorporated the *Project Plan* results, which in turn generated the momentum to establish the NFWS at NAS Miramar, in California. The school's brief was to give US Navy fighter crews rigorous training in ACM. Those who graduated from the courses would then return to their units and pass on the expertise.

The NFWS programme was headed by Lt Cdr Dan Pedersen, the operations officer for co-located F-4 training squadron VF-121. Despite having minimal assets, he assembled a team of five outstanding pilots that had extensive experience of ACM in combat. They immediately set about writing a 300-page syllabus for Topgun F-4 and F-8 students while still flying as instructors and sharing aircraft with VF-121 and A-4-equipped VF-126 (formerly VA-126, which had provided Skyhawks for ACM training since the early 1960s). Lt Cdr Jim Ruliffson, who had fought MiG-21s with VF-21, put together the section on optimum use of missiles, Lt Cdr Mel Holmes from VF-143 focused on the aerodynamic issues associated with aerial combat tactics and Lt Cdr John Nash was assigned the air-to-ground syllabus. In respect to air-to-air tactics, Nash observed;

'Nothing changed from World War 2 apart from distances and

As the US Navy's Pacific Fleet F-4 Replacement Squadron, VF-121 'Pacemakers' received its first F4H-1 in 1960, and the unit continued to use Phantom IIs like this early F-4B-08-MC BuNo 148419 well into the 1970s. This particular example was lost in a May 1963 take-off accident, however. Vietnam experience brought radical changes in VF-121's training programmes, replacing the early 'tail-chase' missile shots with realistic ACM training that eventually formed the basis of Topgun instruction (*US Navy*)

speeds. Most of the manoeuvres were very similar, and accomplished the same thing – barrel rolls, high and low yo-yos, lag pursuit, defensive manoeuvres, etc. We would go back and research techniques recorded from World War 2, for example in Heinz Knoke's autobiography, *I Flew for the Führer*.'

Combat veterans and MiG killing Naval Flight Officers Jim Laing and J C Smith passed on their expertise to F-4 RIOs, teaching them to work closely with their pilot. John Nash described how their experience enabled them to;

'Listen to a pilot's commentary on the target, get a radar lock-on in an ACM environment, get a missile off rather than have the pilot go to boresight mode, point his nose at the target and then lock the target up. The ideal way to acquire the target was in lag pursuit or in off-boresight mode, not pointing at the bogie. Once you were pointing at him you were using up the separation distance in which the missile could perform properly. A reasonable visual range was five to six miles at most. You were not going to fight a guy beyond about four miles, and typically you would need two to three miles in a turning fight. You needed at least that to get a radar missile locked up, timed out and fired.'

The first class of four F-4 crews, drawn from *Constellation*'s CVW-14 (VF-142 and VF-143), assembled in Hangar One at NAS Miramar on 3 March 1969. They learned to push their aircraft to their maximum performance against nimble A-4s (MiG-17 substitutes) or F-8s (flown as MiG-21s). This included driving the aircraft into a turn until buffeting occurred, and then learning to handle that potentially dangerous condition so that they had a small turning advantage over a MiG-21. The AIM-9 was prioritised in the new tactics, and each engagement was carefully analysed in debriefing so that crews fully understood, and remembered, the details of the sortie. Pilots such as John Nash, who often flew adversary A-4s borrowed from VF-126, would make up to three gruelling dogfighting sorties each day, taking on two sections of F-4s consecutively in strenuous 40-minute ACM sessions. He logged an astonishing 350 such sorties in a single year.

Pilots found that they could even improve their ability to see small, distant targets like a MiG-21 through appropriate training. Furthermore, NFWS instructors demonstrated to students that the F-4 was capable of flying manoeuvres at lower speeds that would make an F-8 depart from controlled flight. They also learned that the many losses of F-4s in stall-spin conditions could be avoided if the aircraft was not flown at too high an angle of attack, with ailerons in use rather than only the rudder. Below 10,000 ft, the chances of recovering from that situation were slim. The last week of the course included live missile firing against manoeuvring Ryan Firebee drone targets, giving crews a more direct experience of AIM-9 behaviour than they received in previous training. Topgun soon won further support, and it acquired six A-4Es of its own as adversary aircraft.

Throughout, teamwork between pilot and RIO within the cockpit and between aircraft in the 'loose deuce' section in which two F-4s flew about 6000-9000 ft apart in line abreast, covering each other from aerial attack and each able to engage an intruder, was emphasised and developed. There was usually also some vertical separation between the pair. This formation, used by many air forces, greatly increased flexibility compared with the rigid four-ship 'fighting wing' Tactical Air Command approach which its

USAF Fighter Weapons School defended throughout the war. Instead of indulging in a little ACM with squadron mates when the opportunity arose, US Navy F-4 crews were now given three weeks of solid ACM, with back-up classroom instruction on the science of comparative manoeuvrability for various aircraft types.

The Topgun tuition was equally useful for RIOs, as Steve Rudloff explained;

'When it came to dropping bombs, we had gone to Fallon and El Centro with VF-154, so I was pretty well prepared, more as a semi-bombardier/ navigator than as an actual RIO. I spent most of the time with my eyes out of the cockpit. When I was in VF-92 I was selected to go to Topgun, and it was a fantastic experience – I really locked into it. The RIO's role was really enhanced by Topgun doctrines. We had our role in air-to-air combat much more clearly defined, and a great deal more responsibility was cast on the RIO than we had when I first went through the RAG.'

Among the crews who carefully studied the outcomes of these new training approaches were F-4J RIO Lt(jg) Lynn Batterman and pilot Lt Randy Cunningham of VF-96, embarked in *America* off Vietnam in 1970. Batterman recalled;

'He and I were the only ones to consistently check out and re-read the secret manuals we had on the MiGs (we even had some MiG repair/ NATOPS manuals) and the *Have Drill* and *Have Doughnut* manuals, which were controlled by the skipper, Cdr Al Newman, but any crew could check them out.'

Their combat introduction as 'nugget' crew members had been educative in many ways. Their first combat cruise included a carrier landing where they almost hit the rear of the flightdeck in a 'ramp strike' and a brief but embarrassing landing break and approach towards the wrong aircraft carrier. However, they quickly learned from their errors, and it was clear to Batterman that Cunningham was very focused on scoring a MiG kill from the outset. 'He worked harder than average, and was better than average because of it'. He checked intelligence reports on likely MiG locations before each mission. 'We would bait the MiGs by flying 50 ft or so above the sea and approaching the shore as close as possible, trolling up and down the coast'. Although Batterman left the squadron in 1971, his pilot benefitted further from VF-96's additional training between its 1969-70 and 1971-72 cruises.

The long-term outcome of Topgun was that during the *Linebacker* operations of 1972 the US Navy's kill-to-loss ratio worked out at six-to-one (24 MiGs for four F-4s), while the USAF, continuing its established *Rolling Thunder* air-to-air tactics, shot down 48 MiGs but lost 24 aircraft – a two-to-one ratio. Some USAF Phantom IIs had the unique advantage of Combat Tree IFF interrogation equipment that allowed them to identify MiGs beyond visual range, while the US Navy, which was mainly assigned targets in coastal Route Packages, had better warning and ground control from the offshore 'Red Crown' (the fighter controller's call-sign) radar vessels than the USAF, which was given RPs further inland, where radar coverage could be less effective. However, it was clear that the US Navy's new training regime was the main factor in its superior air combat performance in 1972 when the *Rolling Thunder* kill-to-loss ratio of around 2.41-to-1 would be converted to 12.5-to-1 against enemy fighters.

CHAPTER TWO

BLUE TREES, BANDITS AND BOMBS

VF-21 'Freelancers' deployed its F-4B/J Phantom IIs with CVW-2 throughout the war from March 1965 to June 1973. It scored the US Navy Phantom II's first two VPAF MiG kills in June 1965. VF-154 'Black Knights' joined CVW-2 in July 1966, replacing VF-111's F-8Ds and subsequently making six wartime cruises with VF-21 on board *Coral Sea* and *Ranger*. F-4J BuNo 155763/NE 113 (seen here closest to the camera) was lost in a launch accident on 20 February 1969 (*US Navy*)

As the carefully selected Topgun graduates completed their courses and returned to their squadrons, the 'new wisdom' of aerial combat (actually based on lessons that extended back to World War 1) began to spread through the operational F-4 units. However, there was still some resistance among traditionalists, and it took a few years for the philosophy to prove itself generally.

For 'believers' like VF-96 pilot and double MiG killer Lt Matt Connelly, 'Topgun taught us how to fly the F-4 to its advantage and capitalise on the weaknesses of the enemy aircraft'. As the squadron's weapons training officer, he was closely involved in changing the approach to ACM between the unit's 1969-70 and 1971-72 cruises when;

'The whole squadron was given the Topgun academic syllabus. In addition, we flew tactics hops against Topgun jets, as well as other dissimilar aircraft. We even flew against Air Force F-106A Delta Darts at McChord AFB [318th Fighter Interceptor Squadron]. During our turnaround missile shoot, VF-96 expended the entire West Coast training allowance of missiles! This did not make us popular with the WestPac [Western Pacific] staff, but it later paid handsome dividends.'

Eight of the US Navy's 25 MiG kills in 1972 would fall to 'Fighting Falcons', F-4Js, an achievement also aided by the wealth of *Rolling Thunder* experience within the squadron.

Lt Brian Grant of VF-96, Lt Randy 'Yank' (later 'Duke') Cunningham's frequent wingman, attended Topgun in September 1972;

'Topgun was a turning point for me as a fighter pilot. It provided me and the others with what Cunningham knew instinctively – being able to focus on the development of a multi-bogey, multi-dimensional dogfight in slow motion, predict all the planes' flight patterns and make your own aircraft coincide with a firing solution. Cunningham was a very instinctive fighter pilot and a very brave man who additionally worked harder at his craft, and more often, than any other pilot I have ever known.'

For the record, Cunningham returned the praise, saying of Grant, 'There could simply not have been a better wingman on all the Earth'.

Lt Jerry Beaulier and former USAF airman Lt(jg) Steve Barkley from the first F-4 Topgun class of March 1969, featuring VF-142 'Ghostriders' and VF-143 'Pukin' Dogs' from CVW-14, embarked in *Constellation*, were the first to use the NFWS lessons in combat during the carrier's August 1969 to May 1970 cruise. As a well-integrated crew, they spent considerable time refining their procedures and planning for possible MiG encounters at a point in the war when, as Steve Barkley recalled, 'almost never did anyone lay eyes on a MiG, let alone get within Sparrow range of a bandit'.

The 15 crews from VF-142 flew up to 22 sorties daily in March 1970 – two for each crew, with a spare crew for each mission ready in the cockpit to replace a 'down' aircraft. This routine was performed during a 12-hour period, coordinated with other carrier air wings on *Yankee Station* (the carrier force's patrol area) off North Vietnam. Alert Five flights (aircraft on five-minute cockpit alert to cope with any emergency calls, followed up if necessary by an Alert 15 flight), however, continued over 24 hours during roughly 30 days on station, before the carrier took a six-day break in the Philippines, Japan or Hong Kong.

Routine operations for F-4 crews during this 'in between' period of the conflict included BARCAP flights to defend the carrier force and bombing missions over Laos and South Vietnam, usually at night and often opposed by 37 mm AAA. Steve Barkley remembered, 'AAA could easily be seen at night, and there was enough to be interesting. Occasionally, someone would be hit or shot down, so you didn't want to duel with what you

VF-143 'Pukin' Dogs' deployed with CVW-14 on 11 August 1969 to spend 128 days on the line flying from *Constellation*. The napalm canister on the right TER of BuNo 155890 is more likely to have been converted into a baggage pod, as the aircraft is seen here at NAS Miramar on 2 August, just nine days before embarkation on board CVA-64. This jet completed a second Vietnam War cruise with VF-21 (as 'Lance 106') in 1970-71, flying from *Ranger* (*Author's collection via Norman Taylor*)

Positioning the aircraft in exactly the right place on the catapult track required the pilot to use minimum power, careful nose-wheel steering and to keep a close eye on signals from the plane director ahead of him. He would know that any plane director's formal signals made by using their arms above waist level were intended for him, while those below waist level were for other deck crew. The aim was to taxi the nose-wheels over the catapult shuttle, thus ensuring that the aircraft was correctly positioned for launch. Any minor deviations might be corrected by manpower, as in the case of this F-4J on board *America* in 1970 (*US Navy*)

saw'. F-4J BuNo 155889 from VF-143 had probably fallen to AAA, or to flying-control failure, on 22 November 1969 during a bombing run on the North Vietnamese supply trails network near the Ban Karai Pass. The Phantom II entered a steep dive from which pilot Lt(jg) Herbert Wheeler was unable to pull out. He and RIO Lt Henry Bedinger ejected into an area full of Laotian troops, who quickly captured the latter – handed over to the North Vietnamese, Bedinger was released in March 1973. Wheeler was later recovered by a helicopter, as were the pilots of four of *Constellation*'s A-7As, also lost to AAA over Laos during that cruise.

The end of *Rolling Thunder* encouraged the VPAF to extend its MiG activity beyond North Vietnam by expanding the airfields at Bai Tuong, Vinh, Yen Bai and Dong Hoi, which were all closer to the DMZ. A primary objective in this expansion was the VPAF's long-standing desire to intercept the mighty B-52s on their Operation *Arc Light* bombing missions against supply routes in Laos, although it also enabled the short-ranging fighters to intrude into US air activity over the trails, as Steve Barkley explained;

'We were about three weeks into a line period when a USAF rescue helicopter was shot down in Laos by a MiG-21 staging out of the southernmost airfield in North Vietnam. This was quite unexpected as the North Vietnamese hadn't done anything like this in some time. We found it interesting that they should seemingly thumb their noses at us in this manner.'

The helicopter, a 40th Aerospace Rescue and Recovery Squadron HH-53B Jolly Green Giant (66-14434), was one of three attempting to rescue the crew of F-105G *Wild Weasel* 63-8329, shot down on 28 January 1970 while attacking a SAM site just inside North Vietnam. Two MiG-21s suddenly appeared, and one, flown by ace Vu Ngoc Dinh, fired an 'Atoll' missile at 'Jolly Green 71', which exploded, killing the pilot, Maj Holly Bell, and his five crew members. It was the first MiG incursion into Laotian airspace, and this incident provided a salutary warning to all US aircrew operating in the area. It also reminded TF 77 that effective fighter escort for all *Blue Tree* RA-5C Vigilante and RF-8G Crusader reconnaissance missions was essential. Even more vital was the need for better MiG warnings so that F-4 CAP aircraft had a real chance of intercepting incoming threats. However, MiG pilots usually tried to avoid confrontations with US Navy fighters during the occasional VPAF fighter patrols that were made just north of the DMZ in 1969-71.

Most of the early *Blue Tree* escort missions went unchallenged, but this all changed when the North Vietnamese Army (NVA) began to move substantial air defences closer to the country's borders, as Steve Barkley recalled;

'Our sorties [in 1970] were mainly into Laos and South Vietnam for bombing missions, a lot of BARCAPs and occasionally a *Blue Tree* escort into North Vietnam. *Blue Tree* missions were relatively short and invariably a non-event, as we would sweep through North Vietnam at very high airspeeds, spending only a few minutes over land. There was never any defence by the North Vietnamese except an occasional "paint" by a fire-control radar. We never saw a missile fired.'

This situation changed in 1971.

To meet the new threat, Adm Fred Bardshar, commanding Carrier Division 5, ordered BARCAPs to be set up offshore at low altitude so that they could slip in below enemy radar and catch any MiGs making provocative southern excursions. Early attempts to do so in March 1970 failed because of the difficulty in vectoring the F-4s into a position whereby they could positively identify the targets before opening fire.

On 28 March Beaulier and the heavily moustached Barkley were launched in F-4J 'Dakota 201' (BuNo 155875) as the replacement spare for VF-142 CO, Cdr Ruel E Gardner, in a CAP flight led by the commander of CVW-14 and F-8 MiG killer Cdr Paul Speer. Anticipating a lengthy fighter sweep, they carried three external fuel tanks, two AIM-7Es and three AIM-9Ds. A third F-4J crewed by Lt Cdr Gary Hakanson and Lt(jg) Dave van Asdlen joined the flight, which was vectored onto MiG-21s by PO White on board the destroyer USS *Horne* (DLG-30), the 'Red Crown' radar control ship of the day. At 25 miles range they were cleared to fire AIM-7Es, but Hakanson's radar was inoperative and Barkley's also died as they approached the target, ruling out Sparrow launches. 'I was really disappointed – the perfect set-up for a head-on shot and no radar! I fought it for about five miles and then gave up' recalled Barkley. It was later realised that the radar in Speer's F-4 was also faulty, being limited to a one-mile range.

Beaulier sighted the MiGs 10,000 ft above them and closing. The F-4Js climbed to intercept and the MiGs dived towards them. Beaulier turned behind the lead MiG-21, but his F-4 soon lost energy as he was still carrying his three drag-creating external tanks. The MiG leader launched an 'Atoll' unsuccessfully at Speer's Phantom II and Beaulier went after the second MiG, using a 'lag pursuit' tactic to give him the correct distance for an AIM-9D shot. The missile, despite having a poorly adjusted seeker head, exploded inside the MiG-21's tailpipe. 'We pulled up at the MiGs' "four o'clock" and took a look as the doomed aircraft descended into the cloud below us. We never saw an ejection', noted Barkley. The inexperienced pilot, Pham Thanh Nam was killed in the crash. There could be no public recognition of the F-4 crew's success as the Rules of Engagement (RoE) at the time precluded attacks on MiGs unless they threatened a reconnaissance or BARCAP mission. Eventually, a story was released which suggested that Beaulier's MiG-21 had been attacking an RA-5C when it was intercepted.

Lt Jerry Beaulier (left) and Lt(jg) Steve Barkley (sporting his famous moustache) of VF-142 eagerly examine a congratulatory bottle of champagne, presumably from the carrier battle group commander, after their 28 March 1970 MiG-21 shoot-down. Both men were graduates of the very first Topgun class, and Barkley was a former USAF pilot. Recalling his long-standing partnership with Jerry, he recalled, 'Being a bit older and perhaps more focused on quality and survival, our missions tended to be fairly well planned and "by our book". At that point in the war almost never did anyone lay eyes on a MiG, much less get within Sparrow range of a bandit'. Despite this, they carefully planned their tactics for such an occasion, and flew many BARCAP missions in the hope that they would be able to draw a MiG out over the sea. As they accelerated to intercept two MiGs their radar died. They saw the lead jet fire an 'Atoll' at their CAG's F-4J and miss. Following the second MiG-21 through a series of turns, they got an AIM-9 lock-on and saw two Sidewinders detonate within the fighter's tail area. Inexperienced 921st FR MiG-21 pilot Pham Thanh Nam was killed in this combat (*US Navy*)

The F-4's voracious appetite for fuel made in-flight refuelling essential on virtually all missions, using either a EKA-3B 'Electric Whale' or KA-6D Intruder tanker, or a 'buddy' refuelling store hung under the left wing of an A-7 Corsair II. Fuel shortages usually meant that Phantom IIs were the first to land after an Alpha strike. VAQ-130 EKA-3B BuNo 147658 is refuelling two VA-92 F-4Js on a March 1972 CAP mission off the coast of Vietnam. Aside from providing strike aircraft with fuel, 'Electric Whale' crews could also jam the MiG pilots' GCI and radar control links (*US Navy*)

For the F-4 pilots, a MiG kill was a major accolade, particularly at a time of relative inactivity on the ground. Successful crews were also fêted with specially baked cakes, national publicity and congratulatory meetings with 'senior managers' of the war. Similar recognition for successful attack crews and missions was rare, even though aircraft carriers were essentially platforms for attack aircraft.

There were other close calls during this 'in between' period, including one more for VF-142 in 1971 when its CO, Cdr John 'Smoke' Wilson, pursued a MiG-21 for some distance at 600 knots and 2000 ft over hilly North Vietnamese territory, only to lose radar contact in the ground clutter. The hapless 'Fishbed' pilot was the eventual loser when he tried to alight at Quan Lang airfield, as Cdr Wilson explained;

'When he landed they turned off the runway lights, apparently in fear that I would shoot him on the ground and he ran off the runway. Later, we learned that the plane was destroyed, hence my "lame duck" kill that was never recognised.'

The fleet was given radar protection by PIRAZ (positive identification radar advisory zone), which was established when *Yankee Station* was moved from a position 400 miles offshore to a new location about 150 miles from the North Vietnamese coast to reduce the fuel requirements of strike forces and, accordingly, the aerial tanking requirements, thus increasing sortie rates. This put the ships within range of VPAF aircraft, so a series of radar picket vessels (each escorted by a destroyer) patrolled about 30 miles offshore to track air traffic over the mainland and warn of any opportunist air attack attempts on these warships.

The PIRAZ ships, with their powerful SPS-48 radars, were protected by F-4 or F-8 CAPs. 'Red Crown' cruisers like USS *Long Beach* (CGN-9) and USS *Chicago* (CG-11) also had their own on-board defences in the form of powerful RIM-8H Talos missile batteries that boasted an 80-mile range. This weapon was used to destroy at least four intruding MiG-21s during the conflict, the VPAF trying to attack the PIRAZ ships on five separate occasions. One of these aircraft was brought down in a trap laid on by the warships, with the Talos-armed vessel feigning to leave its station, but secretly returning. The MiG pilot, assuming that he might only face short-ranged RIM-2 Terrier missiles that armed smaller PIRAZ vessels, approached too close to survive. Talos missiles were also used against shore-based radar stations. Obviously, the highly sensitive PIRAZ hair-trigger defences meant that identification of friendly aircraft entering or leaving the zone had to be faultlessly accurate.

Aside from targeting the PIRAZ ships, the VPAF also went after their destroyer and frigate escorts that provided very effective naval gunfire to disrupt the NVA's invasion attempts during the Spring Invasion of 1972.

The most notable of these attacks occurred on 19 April 1972 when a 923rd Fighter Regiment (FR) MiG-17, operating from a forward airstrip at night and flying below the minimum altitude of the Talos missile, hit the *Gearing*-class destroyer USS *Higbee* (DD-806) with a 250 kg bomb, causing a substantial fire and destroying its five-inch gun turret as the vessel sailed about 20 miles offshore. A US Navy Phantom II and eight Corsair IIs arrived overhead minutes later, causing a second MiG-17 to turn away. A direct result of this opportunist attack was the installation of Vulcan 20 mm cannon on ships for air defence situations where missiles could not achieve a lock-on.

FOLLOWING THE TRAILS

Between 1969 and 1971 most of the carrier force's efforts were concentrated on the *Commando Hunt* campaign – the constant 'Laotian Highway Patrol' attempts between November 1968 and April 1972 to reduce the flood of supplies from North Vietnam that were carried along the labyrinthine Ho Chi Minh complex of roads and trails into South Vietnam, Laos and Cambodia. It was the longest sustained air interdiction operation ever conducted. A subordinate programme called *Commando Nail* utilised the all-weather radar bombing capability of carrier-borne A-6A/B Intruders, with A-7s and F-4B/Js sharing the bombing once targets had been positively located and illuminated by flares.

Three mountain passes, the Ban Karai, Mu Gia and Ban Raving, were the only access from Vietnam into the *Steel Tiger* area of the Laotian 'panhandle', and they were constantly under attack as choke-points in the network. The convoys, managed by up to 100,000 drivers, bicyclists and support personnel, mainly moved at night, hiding under forest cover during daylight. Despite more than 700,000 tons of bombs being delivered on real or suspected transport targets by US Navy aircraft, the streams of Polish- and Russian-built trucks were never stopped, although many were hit in vertiginous nocturnal strikes in which F-4s sought to identify and destroy the first and last vehicles in the convoy, trapping the rest for destruction by other bombers.

Gently banking for the camera, VF-96 F-4J BuNo 155787 has a reduced load of Mk 82s and no missiles. *Constellation* finally left the line on 22 June 1972 after an extended cruise for which CVW-9 received a Presidential Unit Citation – only the second award of this kind for a naval unit since World War 2 (CVW-11 embarked in *Kitty Hawk* received a Citation in 1968). In 1972 VF-96 became the first squadron to be awarded the Adm Joseph C Clifton Trophy in consecutive years. 'Showtime 104' participated in three Vietnam War deployments with VF-96 between April 1970 and October 1973 (*US Navy*)

Phantom IIs from VF-92 and VF-96 focused their attack efforts around Vinh, bombing trucks, barges, bridges and storage areas near that city. For two weeks in November 1971 F-4Js from VF-92 and VF-96 took over strike duties from CVW-9's A-7s, which had been temporarily grounded on board *Constellation* because of engine problems.

The Vinh Trans-shipment point was a frequent target as it was the most southerly collection point for war materials before they were dispersed into the elusive trails network on trucks, bicycles and pedestrian carriers. Occasionally, large convoys could be caught moving at night. One CVW-9 pilot found 'more trucks than I could count. Headlights stretched as far as you could see and dispersed into the haze'. Convoys of this size were less common from 1969 onwards. By the end of 1970 it was clear that the Laotian trails campaign was struggling to stop more than a small fraction of the supplies being moved south, and the US Navy's effort was temporarily reduced to save operating costs. Two older carriers, USS *Shangri-La* (CVS-38) and *Bon Homme Richard*, duly replaced the larger, Phantom II-capable supercarriers in TF 77. Ironically, this move coincided with an increase in attacks on Army of the Republic of Vietnam (ARVN) outposts by the NVA at the beginning of May 1970, requiring *America* (with VF-92 and VF-96 embarked) and USS *Oriskany* (CVA-34) to return on station.

More often than not, F-4 pilots flying these armed reconnaissance missions found little of interest, dropping their ordnance on 'suspected' storage sites or jettisoning it into a safe offshore disposal area. Generally, there were often periods of comparative inaction for F-4 squadrons, particularly during the endless BARCAPs, as Bill Freckleton noted in a December 1971 letter home;

'Yesterday, Garry [Weigand, his pilot in VF-111] and I made a low pass over one of the destroyers out in the Gulf. It was at about 50 ft and 450 knots. We went right by at bridge level and no doubt gave the sailors watching quite a show. I was reading "zero" on my pressure altimeter. It did make a monotonous hop fairly exciting though. We alternate between missions over Laos etc., and over the Gulf every week, and from four days ago until next Wednesday we will be flying over water. These hops are 2.5 hours long and the most boring. In the weeks when we have overland missions, the hops are only about 1.5 hours, and a lot more exciting in the sense that your blood pressure is up and you are sweating more.

'On another day, I flew a BARCAP in the northern end of the Gulf, and the weather was clear enough to see the coast of North Vietnam and a little way inland. I could see a lot of fishing junks down there on the water about five miles from shore. The land looked quiet and peaceful, not unlike any other land I've seen from the air. I'll just have to get a camera.'

This idyllic image contrasted strongly with the bombing sorties;

'I flew another bombing mission today near the Laotian/Cambodian border. Again, like so many times in the past, it seems like all we hit were trees and dirt, but who knows?'

When crews were given a pre-planned target, they would sometimes arrive to find that it had already been destroyed, and they would then split into sections for armed reconnaissance. However, there were also some major targets below the 20th parallel, including a massive petroleum and ammunition storage area at Xom Trung Hoa, near Vinh, which was destroyed by three days of bombing by US Navy aircraft, including CVW-9 Phantom IIs. Thereafter, the North Vietnamese were careful to disperse and camouflage their supplies, which in turn meant that the majority of the materiel sent out along the trails now reached its destination.

Around ten per cent of US Navy strikes in Laos for 1969 used *Combat Skyspot* radar bombing, which saw formations of F-4s or A-7s guided by on-board USAF AN/APN-154 radar beacons to their targets, where crews would drop their ordnance from above cloud on a signal from a ground-based radar. Results were notoriously difficult to evaluate as the target was frequently obscured from reconnaissance aircraft by cloud or smoke, and damage assessment by observers on the ground usually had to be relied upon. Despite this, *Skyspot* missions continued through to 1972.

Bombing by flare-light could be a vertigo-inducing experience that may have accounted for a few unexplained F-4 losses. In an effort to reduce the risks associated with these missions, crews were forced to experiment with delivery profiles due to the absence of dedicated USAF flare-dropping aircraft. VMFA-333, on board *America* in 1972, used its own method involving SUU-44/A flare pods, loaded with Mk 24 Mod 4 paraflares and hung on the lower and outboard stations of F-4Js' inboard triple ejection racks, as Maj Gen Paul Fratarangelo described. 'They were carried on the lead F-4, and we dropped our own flares on two-plane tactical reconnaissance missions. I recall several I flew both as lead and wingman, with excellent results'.

Lt(jg) Lynn R Batterman was in VF-96 with future MiG killers Lt Matt Connelly, Lt(jg) Tom Blonski and Lt Randy Cunningham. Describing sorties into the area of Laos designated for *Steel Tiger* operations, he discounted the idea that these missions were often spontaneous reactions to interference by enemy defences. 'Most of the bombing missions were pre-planned, with a FAC on a site to pinpoint the target. Usually, there were four Phantom IIs, and the RIOs' job was to read off airspeed, altitude, dive angle and keep an eye out for MiGs'.

There were also frequent strikes by TF 77 aircraft in the I Corps area, normally managed by the US Marine Corps and extending over five South Vietnamese provinces in the central coastal plain from the DMZ to the south of Quang Ngai – a distance of more than 200 miles. Despite President Richard Nixon's drawdown of US forces in Vietnam in 1969-70, the US Marine Corps' F-4 Phantom II units based at Chu Lai and Da Nang, in South Vietnam, flew record numbers of close air support (CAS) sorties for Marine ground troops, as well as frequent trails attacks by day and night (see *Osprey Combat Aircraft 94 – US Marine Corps F-4 Phantom II Units of the Vietnam War* for further details). Carriers launched small strike

Heavy seas produced extremely difficult conditions on deck and created extra corrosion control work for aircraft maintainers. VF-31 and VF-103 F-4Bs are seen here getting soaked aboard *Saratoga* in the Atlantic in early 1968. Fortunately, such conditions were rarely encountered in the Gulf of Tonkin. Both VF-31 and VF-103 converted to the F-4J in 1968 and deployed to TF 77 four years later. The Alert Five crews had to launch if required in virtually any weather or sea conditions, but these Phantom IIs are securely chained to the deck in this extreme case (*US Navy*)

BARCAP missions were usually considered tedious unless they led to a MiG encounter, but they could present other hazards too. MiG killer Lt Cdr Roy Cash Jr took part in an 18 June 1972 BARCAP over Hon Nieu island near Vinh while a merchant ship was being attacked. Flying at only 1000 ft, his VF-213 F-4J (BuNo 157273) was hit by 23 mm AAA and the wing caught fire. Hydraulic failure and the consequent loss of flying controls forced him and his RIO, Lt Ron J Laib, to eject after flying 100 miles back in the direction of their carrier. A US Navy helicopter took them the rest of the way to *Kitty Hawk*. This VF-154 'Black Knights' F-4J, photographed during *Ranger's* 1969-70 WestPac, bears the 200 series Modex side numbers that the squadron wore for three of its deployments embarked in CVA-61. During these cruises BARCAPs provided VF-154 aircrew with a substantial amount of their flying time. BuNo 153809 switched to VF-21, the sister-squadron to the 'Black Knights', for the 1970-71 WestPac, becoming 'Lance 105' (*US Navy*)

packages rather than major Alpha strikes that involved the entire air wing. They usually consisted of four to six A-7s during a six-hour daylight period and several two-aircraft launches during a six-hour night-time slot, fitting in with other carriers on station. F-4 units would launch in pairs as escorts or with ordnance for armed reconnaissance attacks, although their aircraft lacked the bombing systems that made the A-7 a more accurate attacker.

When F-4s escorted A-7s on longer strike routes into the *Steel Tiger* area of southern Laos, they usually needed three external fuel tanks, which limited the ordnance load to 2000 lb. For fighter crews, the lack of aerial opposition made bombing an inevitable alternative to justify their place in the air wing. Occasionally, F-4s led Alpha strikes later in the war, although this was unpopular with the attack squadrons, many of whom were also sore about the usual awarding of a coveted Silver Star medal to fighter crews for shooting down a MiG, whereas destroying a crucial bridge in North Vietnam with accurate bombing was only worth a less prestigious Air Medal for A-6 or A-7 personnel. As for the relative military value of killing a single enemy fighter pilot set against the deaths of more than 150 NVA troops in a single May 1972 ground attack by four F-4Bs, there were no logical rules to apply.

From March 1968 air operations were controlled by the Da Nang-based Tactical Air Direction Center (DASC), which allotted CAS and direct air support (DAS) missions to 'hot pad' US Marine Corp F-4 units under 1st Marine Air Wing control. Tasking was shared to some extent with US Navy and USAF squadrons when necessary. The combined efforts of the three forces were instrumental in the relief of the Marines' Khe Sanh base in Operation *Niagara*, when aircraft from *Enterprise* contributed to a massive air assault by dropping 1000-lb delayed action bombs on the trenches and bunkers that North Vietnamese troops were digging around the perimeter of the base. According to the carrier's January 1969 Command History, '*Enterprise* planes were soon caving them in as fast as they were dug. Pilots doggedly pursued their combat support missions around the strategically located encampment until the sustained air attack and improved weather conditions managed to break the siege'.

April 1969 brought another change in the order with the establishment of *Defender* station in the Sea of Japan. Following the shoot-down of an EC-121M reconnaissance aircraft from VQ-1 by two MiG-17s from East Tongchongni on 14 April, resulting in the loss of its 31 crew, three carriers were transferred to TF 71 for eight days to provide a show of force off North Korea that comprised 29 ships. The carriers involved were *Enterprise*, with VF-92 and VF-96 embarked as part of CVW-9, USS *Ranger* (CVA-61), with the F-4Js of VF-21 and VF-154 on board as part of CVW-2, and USS *Ticonderoga* (CVA-14), with CVW-16 embarked, which included two F-8 squadrons. A similar naval group had previously been deployed to respond to the North Korean capture of the intelligence gathering vessel USS *Pueblo* (AGER-2) in January 1968.

The pilot of VF-151 'Vigilantes' F-4B BuNo 151013 engages full afterburner moments before accelerating down *Midway*'s bow catapult two with a load of 500-lb bombs during CVW-5's 1971 WestPac cruise. Deck crew who supervised catapult launching were often working within about ten feet of F-4s at full power, which could cause hearing damage at ten times that distance. Their helmets offered minimal noise protection. This aircraft was destroyed by an SA-2 missile during a reconnaissance escort mission near Phu Ly on 27 August 1972, with Lt Ted Triebel and Lt(jg) Dave Everett of VF-151 becoming PoWs (*US Navy*)

Upon the carriers' return to *Yankee Station*, the interdiction missions over Laos continued, together with *Blue Tree* escorts over North Vietnam and a new type of attack mission dubbed 'protective reaction', which was to be allowed in response to any attacks on US reconnaissance flights. These strikes, of which 1000 were flown in 1970 alone, were surrounded by even more complex and constantly changing Joint Chiefs of Staff RoE than aircrew had to endure in *Rolling Thunder*. As Seventh Air Force commander Gen John Lavelle commented, 'We finally found out why there are two crew members in the F-4. One is to fly the airplane and one is to carry the briefcase full of the RoE'.

These instructions were issued in messages, wire signals and no-notice directives that baffled aircrew due to their complexity. For protective reaction strikes, the existing RoE were re-stated by Gen John Ryan (Chief of Staff of the USAF) to the effect that aircraft could 'strike any SAM or AAA site in North Vietnam below 20 degrees north that fired at or was activated against US aircraft conducting missions over Laos or North Vietnam. This authority was limited to immediate protective reaction – no subsequent retaliation was authorised'. The word 'activated' implied that detection by airborne radar homing and warning (RHAW) equipment of a lock-on by a 'Fan Song' SAM guidance radar or a ground control intercept (GCI) radar was sufficient provocation to warrant a response.

Ryan was instrumental in sacking Lavelle because he had allegedly sanctioned the repeated bombing of the NVA force build-up near the DMZ and southern parts of North Vietnam by 'liberally interpreting the rules for protective reaction strikes', and then falsifying the evidence to justify these attacks by reporting active enemy opposition when there had been none.

For *Kitty Hawk*'s squadrons (including F-4J-equipped VF-114 and VF-213, assigned to CVW-11), sorties over Laos far outnumbered those over South Vietnam in 1970, with 1862 Laotian strike and combat support sorties in its 8-29 December 1970 line period compared with just 32 over South Vietnam. By 10 March 1971 *Kitty Hawk* and *Ranger* were setting records with up to 233 strike sorties in (*text continues on page 43*)

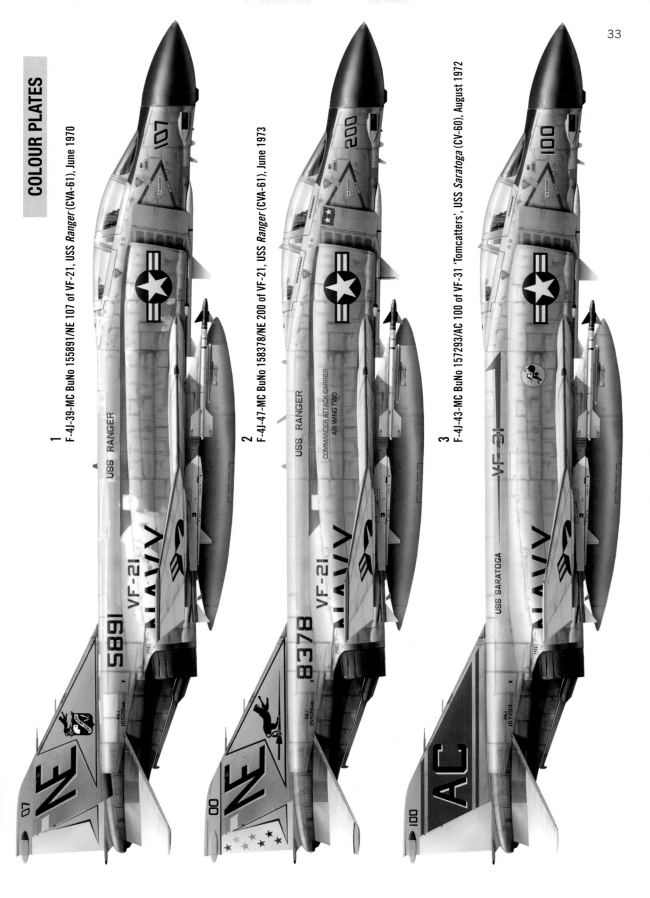

COLOUR PLATES

1
F-4J-39-MC BuNo 155891/NE 107 of VF-21, USS *Ranger* (CVA-61), June 1970

2
F-4J-47-MC BuNo 158378/NE 200 of VF-21, USS *Ranger* (CVA-61), June 1973

3
F-4J-43-MC BuNo 157293/AC 100 of VF-31 'Tomcatters', USS *Saratoga* (CV-60), August 1972

4
F-4J-36-MC BuNo 155864/AC 112 of VF-31, USS *Saratoga* (CV-60), December 1972

5
F-4B-26-MC BuNo 153027/NL 103 of VF-51, USS *Coral Sea* (CVA-43), June 1972

6
F-4B-12-MC BuNo 150417/NL 107 of VF-51, USS *Coral Sea* (CVA-43), August 1971

7
F-4J-29-MC BuNo 153787/AJ 112 of VF-74, USS *America* (CVA-66), April 1973

8
F-4J-34-MC BuNo 155772/NG 213 of VF-92, USS *Enterprise* (CVAN-65), July 1969

9
F-4J-34-MC BuNo 155780/NG 205 of VF-92, USS *Constellation* (CVA-64), 1971-72

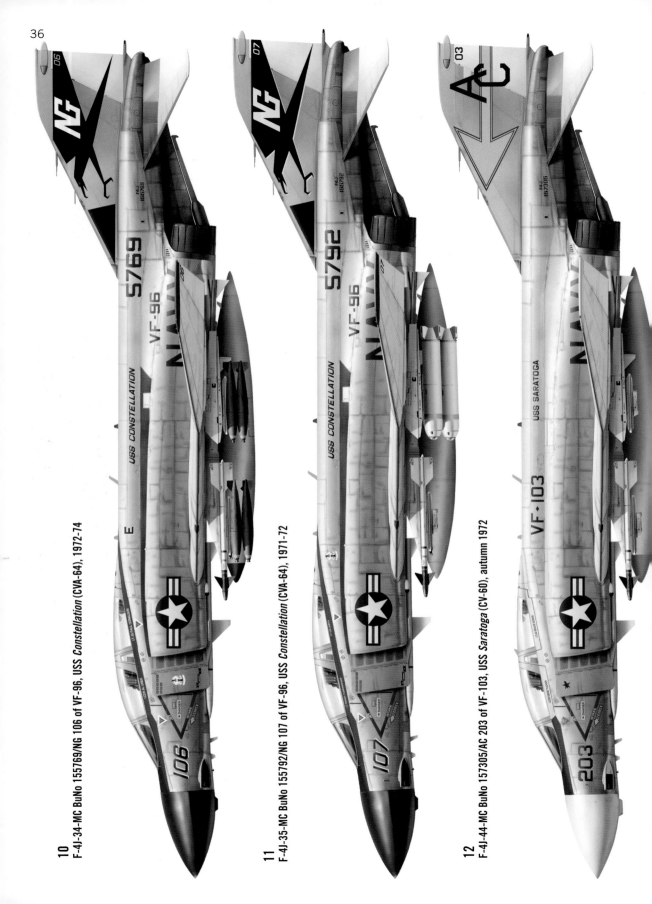

10
F-4J-34-MC BuNo 155769/NG 106 of VF-96, USS *Constellation* (CVA-64), 1972-74

11
F-4J-35-MC BuNo 155792/NG 107 of VF-96, USS *Constellation* (CVA-64), 1971-72

12
F-4J-44-MC BuNo 157305/AC 203 of VF-103, USS *Saratoga* (CV-60), autumn 1972

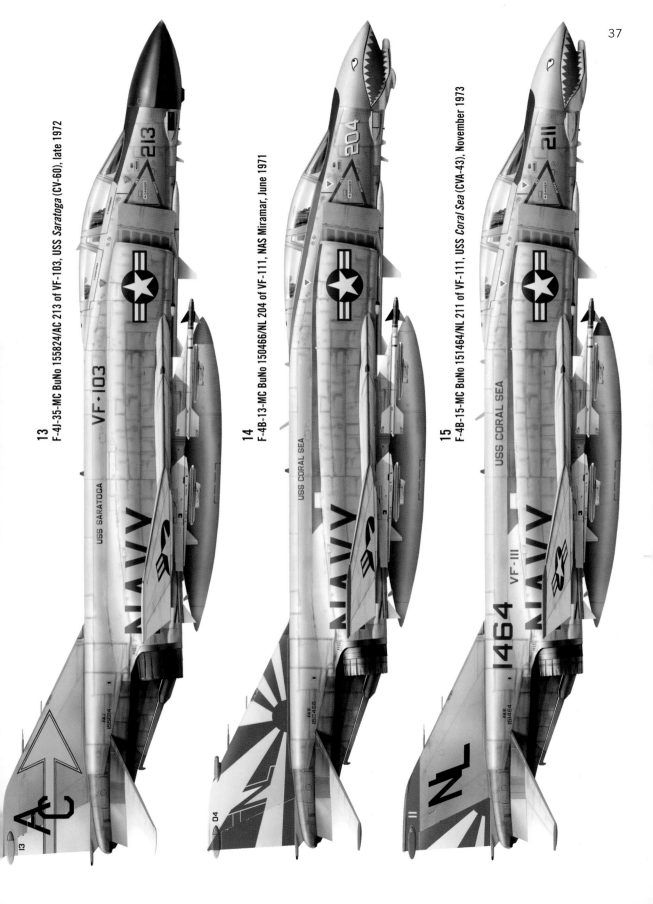

13
F-4J-35-MC BuNo 155824/AC 213 of VF-103, USS *Saratoga* (CV-60), late 1972

14
F-4B-13-MC BuNo 150466/NL 204 of VF-111, NAS Miramar, June 1971

15
F-4B-15-MC BuNo 151464/NL 211 of VF-111, USS *Coral Sea* (CVA-43), November 1973

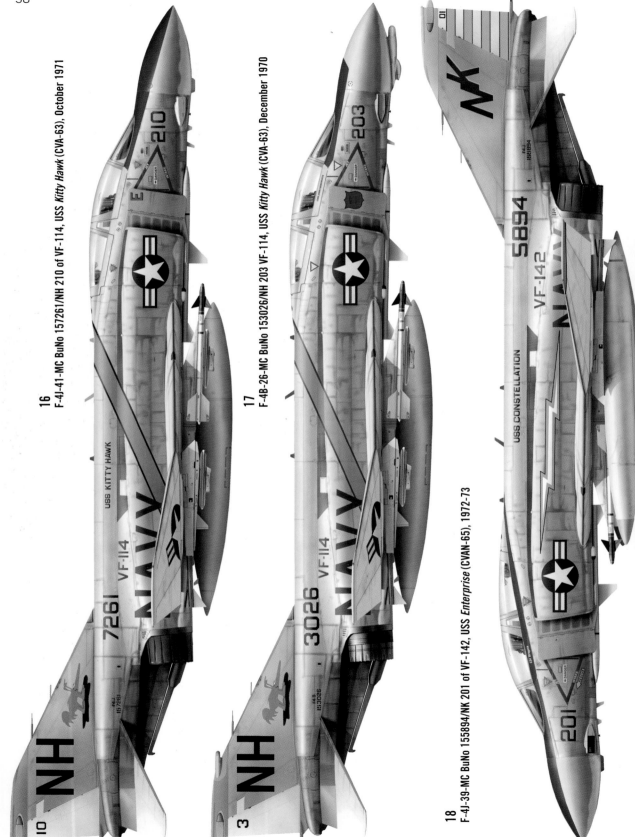

16
F-4J-41-MC BuNo 157261/NH 210 of VF-114, USS *Kitty Hawk* (CVA-63), October 1971

17
F-4B-26-MC BuNo 153026/NH 203 VF-114, USS *Kitty Hawk* (CVA-63), December 1970

18
F-4J-39-MC BuNo 155894/NK 201 of VF-142, USS *Enterprise* (CVAN-65), 1972-73

19
F-4J-34-MC BuNo 155740/NK 211 of VF-142, USS *Enterprise* (CVAN-65), 1972-73

20
F-4B-21-MC BuNo 152239/NK 302 of VF-143, USS *Constellation* (CVA-64), late 1969

21
F-4J-34-MC BuNo 155741/NK 110 of VF-143, USS *Enterprise* (CVAN-65), February 1972

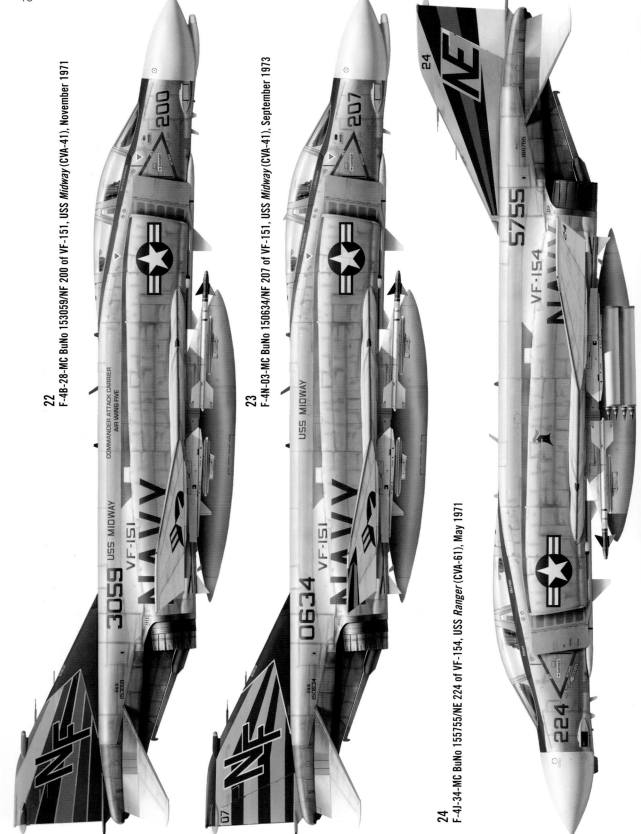

22
F-4B-28-MC BuNo 153059/NF 200 of VF-151, USS *Midway* (CVA-41), November 1971

23
F-4N-03-MC BuNo 150634/NF 207 of VF-151, USS *Midway* (CVA-41), September 1973

24
F-4J-34-MC BuNo 155755/NE 224 of VF-154, USS *Ranger* (CVA-61), May 1971

25
F-4J-46-MC BuNo 158357/NE 210 of VF-154, USS *Ranger* (CVA-61), January 1972

26
F-4B-15-MC BuNo 150996/NF 106 of VF-161, USS *Midway* (CVA-41), 1972-73

27
F-4B-21-MC BuNo 152243/NF 101 of VF-161, USS *Midway* (CVA-41), late 1972

28
F-4J-41-MC BuNo 157272/NH 100 of VF-213, USS *Kitty Hawk* (CVA-64), 1971-72

29
F-4J-40-MC BuNo 157242/NH 102 of VF-213, USS *Kitty Hawk* (CVA-63), May 1972

30
F-4J-36-MC BuNo 155852/AJ 201 of VMFA-333, USS *America* (CVA-66), December 1972

Enterprise's forward deck area, full of CVW-9's aircraft in 1969. The F-4Js of VF-92 and VF-96 are packed tightly alongside RA-5Cs of RVAH-6 'Fleurs' and EKA-3Bs of VAQ-132 'Scorpions'. More Phantom IIs further forward share space with the A-7Bs Corsair IIs of VA-146 'Blue Diamonds' and VA-215 'Barn Owls'. Behind them on the left is a solitary VAW-112 'Golden Hawks' E-2A Hawkeye. Fifteen CVW-9 aircraft were lost in a fire that curtailed the carrier's cruise after only 35 days (US Navy)

While preparing for its fourth combat cruise, Enterprise had an Operational Readiness Inspection at sea some 70 miles from Pearl Harbor on 14 January 1969. The first launch of 16 of CVW-9's 80 aircraft took place, and aircrew headed for their fully armed jets for a second 16-aircraft launch at 0815 hrs. As the engines of F-4J NG 105 from VF-96 were being started by a 'huffer' air-starter, the vehicle's turbine exhaust blasted hot air onto the 15 lb warheads of Zuni rockets mounted on an underwing pylon only 18 inches away. The subsequent explosion ruptured the Phantom II's tanks, sending 2600 gallons of blazing fuel across the carrier's fantail area. Debris holed fuel tanks in other F-4Js and A-7Bs, adding to the horrific blaze. Several 500-lb bombs fell from VF-96 aircraft 105, 103 and 113 and exploded, tearing huge holes in the flightdeck and allowing burning fuel to cascade down through six decks almost to the waterline. Despite loss of water pressure and communications, the crew saved the carrier through heroic coordinated firefighting. Nevertheless, 28 men died, 344 were injured and 15 aircraft were lost, five of them from VF-96 and two from VF-92. Repairs took 51 days to affect, but Enterprise returned to the fight in March 1969 (US Navy)

one day against North Vietnamese targets. Six months later, as part of the expanded 'protective engagement' directive, USAF jets flew 200 sorties against three petroleum tank complexes. Finally, from 26-30 December, the RoE were temporarily modified yet again to allow both USAF and US Navy aircraft to carry out Operation *Proud Deep Alpha*. This saw jets from *Constellation* and *Coral Sea* undertake 423 sorties (out of a total of 1000 flown by US aircraft) against targets below the 20th parallel, but only 75 miles from Hanoi, for five days.

In the first heavy attacks since 1968, fuel depots, forward airfields, SAM sites and vehicle parks were hit, although monsoon weather made target identification difficult and required Alpha strikes to perform radar-controlled bombing. The poor weather also prevented the intended onslaught on MiG airfields from destroying the fighters on the ground. On 30 December VF-111 F-4B BuNo 150418, flown by Lt Cdr David Hoffman and his RIO Lt(jg) Norris Charles, was hit by a SAM – one of 45 fired at US aircraft during the operation. Hoffman was CVW-15's landing signal officer, and he usually helped bring *Coral Sea*'s aircraft safely back aboard. He also flew missions, this being his 205th. Both men ejected as they crossed the coast but they were captured and imprisoned before rescuers could reach them.

Naval aircraft from *Ranger*, *Kitty Hawk* and *Hancock*, guided by USAF forward air controllers, also supported Operation *Lam Son 719* – an ill-fated attempt in February 1971 to capture the massive supply hub at Tchepone and frustrate NVA attempts to invade South Vietnam via bases in Cambodia and Laos. South Vietnamese troops were given the lead in the operation, but it soon became clear that they were generally outclassed by the battle-hardened North Vietnamese forces. The F-4 units provided escort

for these strikes, but focused mainly on their basic reconnaissance escort and deck alert duties.

THE CYCLE

Aircraft carrier decks are among the most dangerous environments, and the disastrous fires on *Oriskany* on 26 October 1966 and USS *Forrestal* (CVA-59) in July 1967, costing a total of 178 lives, were caused by accidents with mishandled live ordnance leading to major conflagrations among aircraft loaded for combat. *Enterprise* suffered similarly during an operational readiness examination at the start of its fourth combat deployment on 14 January 1969 when an LAU-10 Zuni rocket pod loaded on VF-96 F-4J BuNo 155785 was overheated in the exhaust of a carelessly positioned MD-3A 'huffer' jet starting unit during preparations for a practice Alpha strike.

Repeating the incident that began the *Forrestal* fire, the Zuni exploded, rupturing the F-4J's starboard wing external tank and starting a blaze that claimed the lives of 28 men (including the crew of BuNo 155785, pilot Lt(jg) James Berry and RIO Lt(jg) Buddy Pyeatt, whose canopy was jammed by the heat). Fifteen aircraft were also destroyed, including two F-4Js from VF-92 and half of the Phantom IIs assigned to VF-96, at a cost of $56 million.

Fortunately, the ship's crew was preparing for a general quarters situation, meaning that all stations were manned. Also, most of the aircrew got out of their cockpits and retreated to their ready rooms, reducing casualties among their numbers. *Enterprise* retired to Pearl Harbor for six weeks of extensive repairs to two large holes in its flightdeck near the arresting cables and other major fire damage. CVW-9's surviving fighters went ashore to MCAS Kaneohe Bay,

The tailhook of 'Bandwagon 113' – VF-31 'Tomcatters' F-4J BuNo 155843 – catches an arresting wire on board *Saratoga*'s flightdeck. The F-4J's ailerons deflected down by 16.5 degrees when the landing gear and flaps were lowered, and this, combined with the slotted stabilator, reduced the jet's original landing speed of 137 knots by a full 12 knots. The slotted stabilator also reduced the risk of over-rotation on catapult launch. On a standard carrier approach the landing gear was usually lowered at 250 knots and the flaps at 195 knots as the F-4J turned to fly abeam the ship, ready to turn again at 180 degrees and 450 ft and fly on the glide slope to an arrested landing. The half-flap position was used for take-off and flaps could be raised at around 300 ft or 200 knots after the undercarriage had retracted (at a maximum speed of 250 knots) (*US Navy*)

Both of CVW-9's 'CAG bird' F-4Js (BuNo 155799/NG 200 from VF-92 and BuNo 155800/NG 100 of VF-96) undergo pre-launch checks prior to being secured to *Constellation*'s waist catapults in the spring of 1972. A catapult strop is placed in front of NG 200, ready to be attached to hooks beneath its wings, and a hold-back bar to keep the aircraft under tension on the catapult track is lying beneath its engine exhausts (*US Navy*)

LEFT The nose-gear struts of these F-4Js from VF-142 and VF-143 are extended and pilots await the signal to release brakes, advance power and tension the aircraft on the catapult. The control column was then pulled fully aft (except at high gross weights, when over-rotation could occur), the crew placed their heads firmly against the seat headrests and the pilot gave the Catapult Officer a left-hand salute. When the pilot had completed his final power and cockpit checks, a nod to the Catapult Officer was returned by an open hand, five-finger signal and the pilot selected afterburner while holding the control column fully back to deflect the stabilators down (as seen here with NK 204). The catapult then fired unless the pilot shook his head to indicate a 'no go'. At that point the Catapult Officer crossed his forearms over his face and the launch bridle and hold-back bar were de-tensioned ready to remove and replace the faulty Phantom II (*US Navy*)

Hawaii, to recover and re-equip. *Enterprise* returned to action on *Yankee Station* on 31 March 1969.

The risk of death was ever present during deck launch and recovery. Lt(jg) David Neislar of VF-21 was killed when the catapult bridle attached beneath the wings of his F-4J (BuNo 155763) dropped away too soon during the jet's launch, resulting in the nose lowering and the aircraft diving into the sea just ahead of *Ranger* on 20 February 1969. His RIO managed to escape from the sinking Phantom II just before it was run down by the carrier.

Landings, particularly at night, also took their toll. VF-74 F-4J BuNo 153854, returning to *America* in September 1972 after a nocturnal BARCAP, crashed while attempting to land and RIO Lt Michael Rice was killed in an unsuccessful ejection attempt. Sea conditions could also cause losses. Lt Stephen Queen and Lt(jg) Leslie Smith made several attempts to land their VF-96 F-4J on 6 February 1970 with choppy seas below them. When the fuel ran out after they tried, unsuccessfully, to refuel from a tanker they had to abandon their fighter and await a rescue helicopter. Accidents were not confined to fast jets. On 2 October 1969 a C-2A Greyhound supply aircraft with 26 naval personnel on board crashed into the Gulf of Tonkin ten miles short of *Constellation*, the VRC-50 aircraft having taken from NAF Cubi Point, in the Philippines. It was suspected that the Greyhound had suffered some kind of engine problem. There were no survivors.

The F-4 could be surprisingly tolerant at times. Maj Gen Paul Fratarangelo, with VMFA-333 on board *America* in 1972, described a non-standard catapult launch;

'*America* usually shot all F-4s off the waist catapults, but because I was making refresher [night carrier qualification] flights I was taxied to the bow catapults. I went into the "hold back" [the restraining link beneath the rear fuselage] position a little hard and the cat officer signalled a push-back. I raised the flaps for the push-back and everyone (me and the deck crew) forgot to lower them prior to the cat shot. I took the shot at military power [no afterburner]. As soon as the catapult released me my aircraft rotated approximately 60 degrees nose-up. My regular RIO would have ejected, but good ol' "Doc" (the squadron flight surgeon was in the back seat) was just along for the ride. I jammed the throttles to full afterburner and the wonderful J79s responded immediately. I ruddered my F-4 out of wing-rock, raised the gear and when I found the flap handle "up" I realised what had happened. Most Navy guys don't believe this story, saying no-one could prevent an F-4 from going into the water following a no-flap cat shot.'

For F-4 crews, they would divide their routine pre-flight check list between the pilot and RIO. The latter dealt with the weapons system, as Bill Freckleton recalled;

'After electrical power was supplied and the engines had been started, the radar was fired up in the standby mode and the BIT [built-in test] checks – about seven in total – were performed. In the F-4B this included manually tuning the crystals to set radar operating frequencies and monitoring analogue needle indicators to ensure everything was within correct parameters. On the radar scope there was a series of displays that were checked, dealing mainly with the search and track capability of the system. The "steering dot" was checked in relation to the azimuth steering error circle, and other tests were also performed.

'Transmitting power was critical to operation of the radar. We could tweak the pulse video and gain of the radar display to attain an optimum presentation. The Sparrow missiles were tuned on deck then placed on standby until airborne. They would stay tuned and in standby mode until we armed up prior to crossing the beach.'

Naval F-4s had received a series of ECM updates throughout 1967-68 in Project Shoehorn, and these continued into 1974 with the AN/ALQ-126 DECM system for upgraded F-4Bs. With the increased enemy missile threat in 1972, this protection became even more vital, as Bill Freckleton noted;

'The AN/APR-30 RHAW gear worked extremely well. It was BIT-checked on deck prior to each flight and then again airborne. Several times I was able to sight SA-3 "Goa" SAMs by correlating the strobes on the radar warning display to the outside world. This piece of gear wasn't essential in all aircraft as long as one jet in each section had an operable unit. The one piece of gear that was essential was the AN/ALQ-100 deception/repeater. If this was down the aircraft couldn't go "feet dry" [over enemy territory].'

Additional missile checks were usually made after the post-launch meet-up with a KA-6D or EKA-3B (which would have taken off ahead of the strike aircraft), when RIOs would 'lock up'

VF-92's 'Silver Kite 206' (BuNo 155569) awaits orders to taxi forward for a strike mission to deliver its six Mk 82 bombs in late 1971. Safety nets behind the aircraft offered some reassurance to deck crew who could easily be blown overboard by unexpected bursts of jet efflux from stationary or taxiing aircraft (*US Navy*)

Deck crew arrange the recovery of VF-92 F-4J BuNo 155743 following a landing mishap on board *Constellation* during the final stages of CVW-9's pre-deployment work-ups on 18 December 1972. Seat launching rails extending from both cockpits show that the crew ejected. The aircraft, in VF-92's revised 1972 colour scheme, was repaired and subsequently upgraded into an F-4S. A veteran of two previous Vietnam cruises with VF-21, BuNo 155743 was supplied to the 'Silver Kings' as an attrition replacement for BuNo 155797, which was brought down by AAA on 10 May 1972 (*US Navy*)

another jet on radar to check that the latter would work with an actual lock-on to a target. The pilot could also check his AIM-9s by selecting another friendly aircraft's infrared signature and listening for the growling tone from his missile. Caution was obviously necessary during this process.

Launching all 30-35 aircraft in an Alpha package and assembling the formation as it orbited the carrier, while the escort and flak suppression Phantom IIs topped off their tanks, could take up to 30 minutes. As former VF-92 pilot Curt Dosé recalled;

'An Alpha strike launched everything at once, then made a "ready deck" for aircraft as they returned. When they were all back you re-spotted, re-armed and launched the second strike about two hours later. The pilots were not the same for adjacent Alpha strikes since the second strike was briefing while the first was being flown. So you flew the first and third strikes, as I did on 10 May 1972, or the second strike. As fighter pilots, we had the additional responsibility of the Alert fighters. There were always two Alert Five aircraft on or near the catapults with crews in them ready to launch in five minutes. There were two more in Alert 15, with crews suited up in the ready room, and they would head for their fighters when the Alert Five launched. A further pair was designated Alert 30, and they suited up and moved into the Alert 15 slot. This routine was adhered to 24 hours a day any time the carrier was not in port. I slept in the F-4 cockpit as much as I slept in my bunk.'

'I would guess about a third of our flights were BARCAP, with the rest divided between photo escort (five per cent), strike (25 per cent), MiGCAP (20 per cent) and SAM suppression (20 per cent). This changed to match the anticipated threat. On *Dixie Station* [off South Vietnam] we were always just strike or BARCAP, although we always carried four Sparrows and four Sidewinders so we were one button away from being a fighter.

'Our CVW-9 fighters were normally very busy with MiGCAP and flak suppression missions on Alpha strikes. The flak suppressors would go in immediately before a strike, accelerating ahead to engage the initial SAMs with Rockeye, then remaining in the area for follow up and MiGCAP. The assigned MiGCAP would have sectors of responsibility towards all expected air-to-air threat directions. We had wide latitude in these sectors, but had to remain in position to respond to the strike force as needed.'

Air wings arriving in the South China Sea usually began their combat operations with air-to-ground missions in low risk areas to acclimatise crews before they faced the more heavily defended parts of North Vietnam.

TESTING THE FOE

Sometimes the protective reaction envelope was extended and F-4s and attack aircraft were purposely sent into likely target areas to provoke a defensive response and justify a strike, but this was generally discouraged. The incursions by MiGs into Laos and South Vietnam also rapidly increased, and US fighters flew 1933 air defence sorties at the start of 1972 to counter the growing threat and reveal the extent of North Vietnam's military incursions. In the first three months 90 protective reaction strikes were flown – only 18 fewer than in the whole of 1971. Many of these missions were undertaken by US Navy crews operating from *Constellation* and *Coral Sea*.

Lt Cdr Tom Bruyere's VF-142 'Ghostriders' F-4J BuNo 155888 'Dakota 207' takes the emergency barricade on board *Enterprise* in November 1972. Hydraulic or undercarriage failure or a known tyre problem could be among the reasons for opting to 'take the barricade', or in this case AAA damage over North Vietnam. Pilots had to jettison any remaining missiles and lower the tailhook before a barricade recovery. At one point during the approach to the flightdeck their normal view of the fresnel lens 'meatball', the main guide to a safe landing, would have been obscured by the extended stanchions of the barricade apparatus. Clearing the nylon barrier or re-rigging it took 30 minutes, which meant that the rest of aircraft in the strike group had to land first. A barricade landing inevitably caused some damage to the aircraft, but the only alternative was usually ejection alongside the carrier (*US Navy*)

USS *Hancock* (CVA-19), an elderly World War 2-vintage ship whose decommissioning date had to be extended by four years due to a shortage of aircraft carriers for the war, joined the force in January 1972. It had CVW-21 embarked, which included two (VF-24 'Checkertails' and VF-211 'Checkmates') of the final four fleet F-8 fighter squadrons within its ranks. The F-4 had by then replaced Crusaders in two other units (VF-51 and VF-111), and all the official MiG kills claimed by the US Navy in 1972 were credited to Phantom II units. Up until June of that year F-8 pilots led the 'scoreboard' with 22 MiGs and two 'probables', half of which had been credited to the Crusaders of VF-24 and VF-211.

TF 77 ships also remained on *Dixie Station* off South Vietnam, despite naval air strikes continuing at a lower tempo from mid-1969 as US troops were progressively withdrawn from the country. By January 1971 only one carrier remained on station – *Ranger*. Missions into the 'panhandle' region of Laos in Operation *Steel Tiger* also continued, CVA-61 losing three A-7Es (this version replacing earlier A-7A/Bs from April 1970) to ground defences and two VF-21 F-4Js in landing and catapult launch accidents.

For *Enterprise*, returning to *Yankee Station* once again in mid-July 1971 with the Phantom IIs of VF-142 and VF-143 (assigned to CVW-14) embarked, strikes were conducted against infiltration and logistics targets in the *Steel Tiger* area, the eastern Laotian 'panhandle' and Military Region I of coastal South Vietnam. CVAN-65's Command History records that these operations were flown 'in all types of weather conditions, both day and night'. However, many aircrews felt that their missions were often of dubious value, and that they launched on many occasions just to keep up the sortie rate – one of the statisticians' main measures of success in the war. Targets in South Vietnam were often of little value, and ordnance costing huge sums was expended to little effect.

INVASION LOOMS

As America struggled to free itself of the burden of the Vietnam War, by late 1971 it was clear that Hanoi was preparing for a major offensive operation into South Vietnam. A steady increase in the volume of military supplies arriving at Haiphong docks from the USSR and China was accompanied by a huge build-up of forces in North Vietnam and an expansion of the air defence network. Mobile SM-73 launchers for SA-2 'Guideline' missiles, their PR-11B transporter-loader vehicles, ZiL-131 tractor trucks and 'Fan Song' radar units all flooded into the area just north of the DMZ in particular. At the same time, 20 air defence battalions with larger calibre (37 mm to 100 mm) guns were moved into Laos, severely threatening protective reaction strikes. When they were joined by eight SAM battalions, all US air activity, including B-52 *Arc Light* missions, was at risk.

The supply effort also accelerated. In 1971 Hanoi ordered 6000 trucks from the Soviet Union, double the previous year's order. From November 1971 to February 1972, 200 SAMs were fired at US aircraft – ten times the number in the same period a year before as the North Vietnamese sought to disguise their elaborate preparations for invading South Vietnam. Many 'Spoon Rest', 'Bar Lock' and 'Whiff' ground interception radars were also moved south and networked with the SAM and AAA systems. These radars could not be monitored by the RHAW equipment in Phantom IIs and other aircraft, and the fact that they were therefore 'activated' (under the RoE) all the time had been one of Lavelle's justifications for increased protective reaction missions. He therefore encouraged squadrons to prepare likely targets, and appropriate bombing tactics for them, well in advance of each mission, rather than merely responding to ground fire opposition spontaneously.

In January 1972 the effort diminished markedly, with only eight sorties being launched over South Vietnam. The sortie rate then increased rapidly to 733 in February in response to increased North Vietnamese activity ahead of an anticipated series of communist attacks that might well have re-enacted the destructive and politically disastrous Tet Offensive of January 1968. It declined once again to only 113 sorties in early March when no such NVA thrust materialised.

This unusual rear view of VF-21 F-4J BuNo 155892 on a TF 77 mission from *Ranger* in 1971 gives some sense of the limited rearward view from the cockpit. Visibility from the cockpit of a MiG-21 was poorer still, but in the estimation of Topgun instructor Lt Cdr John Nash, it was 'not a lot worse than the F-4, and not nearly as bad as people said' (*US Navy*)

CHAPTER THREE

THE FIGHT TO LEAVE

Reflecting on one of his *Rolling Thunder* cruises, VF-96's XO, Cdr Carroll Myers, commented, 'We fighter types had spent most of the cruise on those boring BARCAPs and FORCECAPs [patrolling over the strike force, essentially as an escort]. We were hungry for a MiG!' The massive increase in North Vietnam's war effort in 1971-72 would provide ten F-4 units, and VF-96 in particular, with many opportunities to fulfil this ambition.

After several false alarms earlier in 1971, the Spring Invasion was finally launched following the breakdown of the tenuous peace negotiations in Paris on 23 March 1972. It involved 30,000 NVA troops with hundreds of T-54, PT-76 and T-34 tanks, artillery and considerable anti-aircraft defences, including SA-2s and shoulder-launched SA-7 'Grail' missiles, crossing directly through the DMZ into South Vietnam. The introduction of the SA-7 ground-to-air heat-seeking missile was a real threat to low-flying aircraft. For F-4 crews it meant avoiding the use of afterburner when pulling up from attacking a ground target.

The unprepared Saigon regime had only assumed the possibility of flanking attacks via Laos and Cambodia, as in the 1968 Tet Offensive. It had not planned for a direct invasion across the 20th parallel. Recently trained South Vietnamese troops and the limited US ground forces still in-country had to respond urgently. TF 77 squadrons, initially from *Coral Sea*, *Kitty Hawk* and *Hancock*, and soon reinforced by *Constellation*, were

F-4B BuNo 152278 of VF-111 'Sundowners', refinished with a later style of serial presentation and very few maintenance stencil markings. The '-01' Modex (as in 201 here) was usually reserved for the squadron commander's jet. VF-111's distinctive 'sharksmouth' nose marking was adopted in 1963 during its F-8D Crusader period under the leadership of Cdr Charles E Ray, and it remained in place on subsequent F-4s, F-14s and its current equipment, the F-5 Tiger II (as VFC-111). The unit's 'Sundowners' title originated in Hawaii prior to the squadron, as VF-11, going to fight the Japanese at Guadalcanal in 1943 in F4F Wildcats. It reflected the idea of shooting down Japanese 'suns' (expressed later in the sunset tail design) and also the term 'downer', which in naval parlance meant a diligent sailor whose captain might hand out a grog ration when the sun went down below the yardarm (*US Navy*) vital components in a rapidly enlarged naval force that began to provide urgently needed air support for the ARVN as it was gradually forced to retreat southwards. Reintroduction of substantial US ground forces was politically impossible for Richard Nixon, but the short-notice availability of carriers and offshore heavy gun platforms provided a vital 'surge' capability.

Midway arrived in the Gulf of Tonkin on 21 April and two US Marine Corps F-4B squadrons had been flown into Da Nang 16 days earlier, these units immediately beginning an intense CAS effort. In the first week of April alone, 680 sorties were launched from TF 77 carriers – a ten-fold increase on the total in the previous three months, although a persistent thick overcast severely limited aerial attacks on NVA troops for the first two weeks of the invasion, and no strikes were permitted north of the DMZ. Much of the naval action came instead from heavy gunfire, with TF 77 deploying groups of three destroyers and cruisers relatively close inshore. Sixteen vessels were in turn hit by fire from NVA shore batteries in 1972. Naval gunfire remained a vital factor in limiting North Vietnam's incursion throughout the rest of the war.

In Washington DC, urgent plans were made to reinforce the carriers further so that seven CVA vessels were available by June, as the majority of US ground forces (more than 400,000 troops) and much of the USAF air power in-theatre had by then been withdrawn. Naval air forces, therefore, took on the majority of the ground attack effort during this period.

Meanwhile, the VPAF's MiG force had expanded to include more than 250 fighters. MiG-21s were concentrated at Kep, Yen Bai and Hoa Lac air bases, with GCI support from the 26th, 43rd and 45th Radar Companies. Pilots of the 921st FR had converted to the MiG-21MF 'Fishbed-J' with the much-improved RP-22S Sapfir-21 air interception radar, AA-2B semi-active missiles, GSh-23L gun pack and a very effective ASP-PF-21 lead-computing gunsight. A second MiG-21 unit, the 927th 'Lam Son' FR, was established in February 1972 with the earlier MiG-21PFM, while 31 supersonic MiG-19S (Shenyang J-6) fighters had been operational with the 925th FR since February 1969.

All US Marine Corps tactical aircraft, including F-4s, had also been withdrawn from the area by December 1971, but three squadrons returned to Da Nang in April 1972. In the first three months of 1972 the US Navy had a daily rate of only 1.4 carriers on station (with duties shared between *Coral Sea* and *Constellation*), rather than the three deployed a year previously. CVW-9's A-7 squadrons had also become the first TF 77 units to employ laser-guided bombs during CVA-64's 1971-72 cruise, the US Navy being keen to emulate the success the USAF had so far enjoyed with the weapon. Problems in generating suitable target illumination from a carrier-based laser-carrying aircraft delayed further air wing use for several years, however.

The TF 77 force in the Gulf of Tonkin was briefly reduced in size in mid-December 1971 when *Enterprise* left the line temporarily to provide a show of force in the Indian Ocean during the Indo-Pakistan war.

Coral Sea's deployment in 1971 saw some changes in its CVW-15 complement, including five new fighter and attack units. VF-51 'Screaming Eagles' and VF-111 'Sundowners', previously F-8 Crusader units with CVW-5 and CVW-8, respectively, received some rather elderly F-4Bs, dressed in eye-catching squadron decor – these units replaced VF-151 and VF-161, which had been transferred to CVW-5. CVW-15's usual E-2A AEW aircraft (flown by VAW-116) were replaced by war-weary E-1B Tracers (of VAW-111 Det 4), with their massive 'Stoof' Hazeltine AN/APS-82 radomes, due to a shortage of Hawkeyes.

As the VPAF had forward-deployed flights of MiGs to primitive airfields at Vinh, Quan Lang and Bai Thuong, the presence of F-4 units to protect *Coral Sea's* interdiction and reconnaissance efforts over Laos was increasingly vital. Together with *Constellation's* CVW-9, CVW-15 flew 423 interdiction and reconnaissance sorties in the last five days of December 1971 as part of the joint USAF/US Navy Operation *Proud Deep Alpha*. The main aim of this venture was the destruction of forward airfields like Bai Thuong and Quan Lang (that were a threat to B-52 flights), as well as attacks on other supply and logistics targets south of the 20th parallel. A protective reaction strike by *Kitty Hawk's* CVW-11 for a *Blue Tree* RA-5C caused the 'incidental destruction' of two MiG-21Fs that were standing on strip alert at Quan Lang in April 1971.

When *Enterprise* returned to *Yankee Station* on 18 January following its brief Indian Ocean diversion, CVW-14 resumed protective reaction strikes the following day. *Constellation* had begun the third line period of its 1971-72 cruise eight days earlier, and a strike on 19 January encountered VPAF fighters, resulting in the first MiG kill since Beaulier and Barkley had enjoyed success in March 1970.

The mission was generated in response to SA-2 launches and AAA fire at an RA-5C as it reconnoitred Quang Lang airfield, from where MiG-21s had made several attempts to intercept B-52s by popping up from very low altitude under night-time ground control, firing missiles and then diving back into the 'weeds' to avoid F-4 escorts. The airfield was heavily defended and the MiGs were hidden in caves. Approaching the target from Laos, the 35-strong protective reaction strike force of A-6As, A-7Es and F-4Js was prepared to hit the airfield from three directions if the RVAH-11 'Checkertails' RA-5C sent to fly over the base ahead of the jets was fired upon. If the Vigilante was not engaged, the CVW-9 aircraft would immediately return to *Constellation*.

Lt Randall Cunningham and his RIO Lt(jg) William 'Irish' Driscoll in the MiGCAP flight, manning F-4J BuNo 157267 'Showtime 112', soon saw ECM warnings in the cockpit of their jet and 57 mm AAA rising towards them and their wingman in the MiGCAP element, Lt Brian Grant and his RIO, Lt Jerry 'Seacow' Sullivan. There were several SAM firings shortly thereafter, forcing the sophisticated $14m RA-5C and the MiGCAP F-4Js to make maximum-g turns to escape two of them. As Brian Grant recalled for this author;

VF-92's 'CAG bird' F-4J BuNo 155799 flies in close formation with RVAH-11 RA-5C BuNo 156614 (which later had unique 'sharkmouths' markings added to its cavernous air intakes) in 1972. Aircraft from both units flew many 'low and fast' *Blue Tree* reconnaissance missions together. 'NG 604' subsequently flew with RVAH-3 and RVAH-6 until it was lost whilst serving with the latter unit on 11 July 1974. The aircraft suffered an uncontrollable engine fire shortly after launching on a night mission from *Forrestal* in the Mediterranean (*US Navy*)

'The mission was the first time I was opposed by SAMs. The first missile was a very close call and the remaining two or three diverted my attention from Randy Cunningham to the point where I lost sight and did not regain formation until after the kill.'

Cunningham estimated that 18 SAMs were fired at them, and he had to evade three at once, losing much of his aircraft's energy through a series of strenuous manoeuvres and barely recovering.

As the attack aircraft went about devastating the SAM sites with Mk 20 Rockeyes and cratering the runway with 1000-lb general purpose (GP) bombs, Cunningham noticed what seemed to be two A-7Es exiting the target area at very low altitude – an opinion he soon revised when he noticed their silver finish and afterburning engines, neither of which were characteristics of the Corsair II. He quickly turned to follow the two MiG-21MF 'blue bandits', which were at an altitude of just 200 ft and travelling at 650 knots. Although Driscoll announced that he had a radar lock-on for an AIM-7E-2 launch, Cunningham distrusted the missile and turned to HEAT on his missile selector switch for an AIM-9 shot. Releasing the missile directly behind the MiG, he was disappointed to see the VPAF pilot (Nguyen Tu Dung) make a maximum-g turn and evade the Sidewinder.

'Duke' Cunningham's speed enabled him to turn after the MiG, whose wingman chose to leave the engagement at that point. 'Showtime 112' was by now inverted at 200 ft and 500 knots, and Cunningham made a fast aileron roll to return to a firing position, waiting for the MiG to reverse his turn before firing a second AIM-9G. It struck the 'Fishbed', some 3700 ft ahead of the F-4, just as it levelled its wings in afterburner, blowing off the rear half of the fuselage and reducing the rest to a fireball that spread over the ground near a small village. Cunningham then set off in pursuit of the other MiG-21 as it headed for Bai Thuong 'on the deck', firing an AIM-7E-2 at extreme range. The missile failed to leave the aircraft and the MiG-21MF, with powered controls for better low-altitude handling, escaped as 'Showtime 112's' fuel gauges indicated an urgent need for a 'buddy' tanker A-7.

This first aerial success of 1972 proved the lessons of Topgun, absorbed by Cunningham during a temporary staff secondment to the unit ahead of his first WestPac deployment on board *America* in 1970.

Operation *Proud Deep Alpha* took *Coral Sea* into intense action during its sixth combat deployment, which inflicted 16 combat and operational losses (including three F-4Bs) on CVW-15, but also brought five MiG-17 kills for its two Phantom II squadrons. The first of these fell to VF-111 crew Lt Garry Weigand

Virginian Lt Garry 'Greyhound' Weigand, one of the many ex-F-8 pilots in VF-111 after the unit switched from the Crusader to the Phantom II, was teamed with Lt(jg) Bill 'Farkle' Freckleton, born in Scotland and raised in California in a Navy family. As a 'Sundowner' crew from 1970, they flew 110 missions together and scored the squadron's only MiG kill in an F-4. It occurred during a *Blue Tree* strike on 6 March 1972 that had the covert purpose of trolling for MiGs. Without a working radar, Weigand and Freckleton employed some effective visual teamwork and dogfighting tactics to down Hoang Ich's MiG-17 with an AIM-9 (*US Navy*)

and Lt(jg) Bill Freckleton, who were part of a FORCECAP section led by Lt(jg)s Jim Stillinger and Rick Olin on 6 March 1972. Weigand was a frequent wingman choice for Cdr Jim Ruliffson, one of the principal figures in the establishment of Topgun who had subsequently become a flight leader in VF-111. He and 'Farkle' Freckleton were to complete 117 combat missions together. The 6 March mission was to protect a *Blue Tree* reconnaissance flight over Quang Lang airfield by maintaining an offshore orbit around *Chicago*, the 'Red Crown' radar control ship of the day.

'My radar was "down" prior to the launch', Bill Freckleton explained. 'I had no search or track capability, so I knew we were "Sidewinder only". Sometimes it was possible to revive a radar set.

'We always hoped that by recycling the system from "on" to "off" and back on again, then running BIT checks, that the radar would magically cure itself. Sometimes this procedure worked. In a combat situation you would try anything to get a full "up" and operational radar. Sometimes putting "g" on the aircraft would bring a dead radar back to life. Occasionally, the wave-guides would have a leak and could not maintain the required pressure for radar operation. In those cases the transmitter would not work above a certain altitude due to lack of pressurisation, which meant we either stayed low with an operable radar or went high with no radar.'

The F-4B's pulse-only Aero 1A radar/fire control system had more basic self-checking methods than the pulse-Doppler AN/AWG-10 in the F-4J.

The lead fighter controller on board *Chicago* on 6 March was Chief Radarman Larry H Nowell, who was ultimately credited with guiding US fighters to successful MiG engagements on 13 occasions. Despite the restricted visibility from the back seat of his F-4B 'Old Nick 201' (BuNo 153019), Bill Freckleton kept a close watch for MiGs, finally detecting a MiG-17 to their left as they descended through 8000 ft. Stillinger moved to pursue and quickly became involved in a turning fight, which he began to lose. He decided to 'bug out', heading away straight and level at high speed and very low altitude, with the 921st FR MiG flown by Hoang Ich in pursuit, afterburner blazing. Garry 'Greyhound' Weigand took the chance of a Sidewinder tail shot at an altitude of 500 ft and the MiG broke in two before it crashed into the forest.

Sister-squadron VF-51 contained a group of highly competitive ex-F-8 pilots commanded by Cdr Foster Teague who were 'hungry for MiGs'. However, the unit lost its senior RIO, Lt Cdr James B Souder (on his third combat tour and 335th F-4B combat mission), with 'nugget' pilot Lt Al Molinaire to a MiG-21PFM flown by Hoang Quoc Dung on 27 April 1972, prior to the squadron downing the first of four MiG-17s.

Armed with air-to-air missiles and Rockeye as wingman to Cdr 'Tooter' Teague and Lt Ralph Howell, Molinaire and Souder had destroyed a truck en route to their bridge target near Vinh earlier in the mission. Souder received information that a single MiG-21 from Phuc Yen was closing directly on them below a thick cloud layer near Bai Thuong airfield while the VF-51 jets maintained an 8000 ft altitude. He speculated that the MiG pilot might have known he was intercepting an F-4B 'which didn't have the pulse-Doppler radar with look-down capability, or he would not have been so foolish as to come right at us like he was'. As the MiG

James B Souder, a great champion of the importance of the RIO, joined VF-143 in March 1966 and he was in the back seat of the F-4B flown by the unit CO, Cdr Dave Grossheusch, when technical faults denied them a MiG kill in October 1966. Their wingmen, Lt(jg)s Bob Hickey and Jerry Morris, made the kill instead. By 27 April 1972 Souder had completed 325 combat missions and transferred to VF-51. On that day he flew a TARCAP with inexperienced pilot Lt(jg) Al Molinaire, and while orbiting near Bai Thuong there was some confusion over the position on radar of a MiG heading towards them. They were duly jumped by Hoang Quoc Dung in his MiG-21PFM, which had not been detected visually. The VPAF pilot fired an 'Atoll' from a range of two miles, the missile hitting the F-4B and knocking out both of its engines. Souder and Molinaire ejected shortly thereafter, and both men became PoWs (*US Navy*)

Lt(jg) Al Molinaire and Lt Cdr J B Souder were flying this F-4B (BuNo 153025) when they were hit by an 'Atoll' on 27 April 1972. Souder advised his pilot to fly the jet for as long as possible, despite a raging fire and severe damage to the engines. As he judged the situation, 'My studies of F-4 shoot-down reports instantly came back to me, and I knew the Phantom II had a reputation for not exploding even when it was burning badly, if it had not exploded upon first being hit'. The crew had to eject when the aircraft's tail eventually burned through and fell off. BuNo 153025 had previously served with VF-213 prior to joining VF-51 (*US Navy*)

approached within 30 miles, still below thick cloud and in ground clutter, Souder decided that 'It was getting to be time to start looking with the radar. A MiG-21 is a little plane and it has a tiny radar signature, so it would have been useless to be searching for him before then'.

At 20 miles range 'I searched all over but couldn't find the MiG' and at four miles Souder 'abandoned the radar' and resorted to a visual sweep, at which point he suddenly received the unwelcome news from 'Red Crown' that the MiG 'might have slipped behind you', followed by a loud concussion in the rear of his Phantom II (BuNo 153025 NL 102) as an 'Atoll' took out both engines. 'I was thrust forward in my ejection seat straps, and it felt just like when you are going at supersonic speed and you come out of afterburner'. A glance in the cockpit mirrors showed Souder that the entire rear fuselage was blazing, and he tried to get Molinaire to head towards high ground, where rescue might be easier.

As he saw the MiG appear ahead of them, Souder's impulse, based on a long-standing desire to get a MiG, was to re-engage the radar that he had already stowed away ready for his ejection and try a last-minute missile shot at his adversary, but Al Molinaire, who was trying to reach the coast, announced that he was about to lose control of the F-4B as the hydraulics drained out. They left the crippled fighter as it began a slow roll to the right at 3000 ft and were soon captured and imprisoned in Hanoi, albeit for less than a year before release.

Eight weeks earlier, on 6 March, Cdr Teague and RIO Lt Ralph Howell had had the chance to down a MiG-17 when an RA-5C crew covering a strike on Quang Lang airfield reported several enemy jets over the target area. Teague and his wingman headed off to intervene in F-4B BuNo 150456 NL100, later to become a MiG killer for 'Devil' Houston and Kevin Moore, and saw a MiG-17 to their left. Teague fired an AIM-9 at it and watched debris flying from the fighter's tail area. He then went after another MiG-17 flying above him. By then Teague's wingman, Lt David Palmer, had left the scene as his radio was inoperative, but luckily RIO Howell was the 'built-in wingman' and detected another MiG-17 right on their tail and firing at them.

Teague had often flown the MiG-17 during *Have Drill* and he understood it well. He used his superior speed to separate from the engagement and climb vertically, returning behind the MiG. Unfortunately, he fired his next Sidewinder from too short a range and had to watch it zoom past the fighter's canopy without exploding, allowing the enemy pilot to make a hasty 180-degree reversal and escape. He went after yet another MiG-17 but had to let it go when a fourth 'Red Bandit' turned towards him. Teague and Howell then had to leave as fuel was now running low, and they subsequently failed to receive a kill credit for the first MiG they hit, although a 'Fresco-C' was later reported to have landed at Quang Lang with major damage.

Operation *Freedom Train* began on 5 April and extended into May in Operation *Fresh Bath* as an accelerated attempt to curtail the long-anticipated invasion of South Vietnam and intensify the destruction of the North's re-supply routes and war materials. The aerial assault moved just north of the 20th parallel, with carrier-based aircraft also supporting the USAF's *Freedom Porch* B-52 attacks on fuel dumps in the Haiphong port area. Further south, F-4 bombers within carrier air wings struck targets at An Loc, close to Saigon.

North Vietnamese troops pick over the remains of 'Screaming Eagle 102' after the 27 April 1972 shoot-down which consigned Al Molinaire and J B Souder to 11 months of PoW incarceration. Souder had already completed 325 missions with VF-143 and VF-51 by the time he was captured. Loss rates for US Navy F-4s ran at 0.7 per 1000 sorties, compared with 1.4 for A-6 Intruders and 1.0 for A-4 Skyhawks, which were generally more exposed to SAMs and AAA. Carrier-borne F-4 squadrons usually had 12-13 aircraft on strength (*István Toperczer*)

For the first time since the conflict had commenced, there was some relaxation in targeting in response to the massive NVA assault and Hanoi's willingness to engage in large-scale land warfare with tanks and artillery. Richard Nixon, fiercely opposed to communism and infuriated by this blatant attempt to take over South Vietnam, stated (off the record) that 'the bastards have never been bombed like they are going to be bombed this time'. This was a prediction of his all-out assault on Hanoi at the end of 1972. Such a threat would have made little difference to North Vietnamese resolve to occupy South Vietnam even if its leaders had heard his warning. They accepted the loss of around 100,000 troops in the Spring Offensive, half of them killed by air strikes.

Most of the F-4 missions still concentrated on strike and escort, with flak suppression more frequently scheduled as the opposing air defences intensified. Brian Grant was involved in a number of these often dangerous missions;

'Strike and flak suppression employed the same 40-degree dive angle. Entry [to the dive] was at about 12,000 ft and pull-out was above 3500 ft or so to avoid the predicted bomb fragmentation pattern. Mk 20 Rockeye IIs were used for flak suppression, loaded two on each bomb rack for a total of four. We delivered all of them in a ripple for a more even spread. The F-4J had an "iron cross" fixed gunsight, with "mil" depression depending on the weapon carried or the dive angle. It was fairly accurate, but due to more limited training in bomb delivery I can take an educated guess that our average fighter pilot's CEP [circular error of probability, a measure of bombing accuracy] was 150 ft, maybe 100 ft on a good day. The A-6 and A-7 squadrons probably attained 50 to 75 ft CEP.'

As the MiG threat increased so did the need for missiles. Bill Freckleton of VF-111 remembered, 'We were always configured with both AIM-7s and AIM-9s whenever we were on an interdiction or air defence mission. We even carried both missiles when we were loaded with six Mk 82 500-lb bombs for a strike mission'.

MAYHEM IN MAY

Public impatience over America's continued costly support for the failing South Vietnamese government compelled President Nixon to continue his drawdown of ground troops, placing an increased reliance on air power to fulfil his defence obligations to Saigon. A new campaign of air attacks on North Vietnam was also discussed in detail. USS *Saratoga* (CVA-60, which was re-designated CV-60 on 30 June) departed from Mayport, Florida, on 11 April for its only WestPac cruise. It had CVW-3 embarked, which included the F-4Js of VF-31 'Tomcatters' and VF-103 'Sluggers'. *Midway* had set out from Alameda, California, the previous day, returning to battle for the third time and making its second cruise with VF-151 and VF-161 embarked as part of its CVW-5.

An unprecedented period of air-to-air successes for US Navy Phantom II squadrons began 6 May, with 16 out of their total of 26 MiG kills in the year from January 1972 occurring in a 20-day period. In May USAF F-4s also accounted for 11 MiGs, which, together with the destruction of others on airfields, constituted the sort of serious attrition of VPAF strength that US pilots had hoped to inflict since the beginning of the conflict. In that month TF 77 had its Vietnam War maximum of six carriers on station with ten squadrons of F-4B/Js – VF-51 and VF-111 on board *Coral Sea*, VF-151 and VF-161 on board *Midway*, VF-92 and VF-96 on board *Constellation*, VF-31 and VF-103 on board *Saratoga* and VF-114 and VF-213 on board *Kitty Hawk*, together with *Hancock*'s two very successful F-8J units, VF-24 and VF-211.

All of them were eager for an aerial victory, although many of their missions would as usual involve duties that did not put them in potential contact with enemy fighters. After his MiG kill, Jerry Houston recalled, 'As happy and self-content as I was upon returning to the ship, it was also an embarrassing moment because I knew how desperately everyone else wanted their own MiG'.

Coral Sea's VF-51 'Screaming Eagles' destroyed the first of three MiGs to be lost on 6 May when large Alpha packages were sent against targets like Bai Thuong, where substantial numbers of VPAF aircraft had been detected. A VF-51 TARCAP with Lt Cdr Jerry Houston and Lt(jg) Kevin Moore, in F-4B BuNo 150456, paired with Lt Cdr Chuck Schroeder and RIO Lt Rick Webb, covered a VMA(AW)-224 A-6A Intruder-based Alpha strike led by Lt Cdr Jim Ruliffson in a VF-111 F-4B. The flak suppression Intruder flight was led by CAG Cdr Roger 'Blinky' Sheets, formerly

VF-114's F-4J BuNo 157248 'Linfield 214' chained securely to *Kitty Hawk*'s deck in 1972. Deck crew had to 'spot' aircraft close to the edge of the flightdeck in order to maximise space, often adding to the hazards of working on them in that situation. VF-114 was one of the first US Navy Phantom II units, making two wartime cruises with F-4Js in 1970-72 following four with the F-4B, and it shot down five MiGs during that time. When US Navy F-4s were challenged by MiGs they tended to be MiG-17s from the 923rd FR based at Kep, 30 miles northeast of Hanoi, although they also tangled with MiG-21s from the 921st FR at Phuc Yen (Noi Bai), closer to Hanoi, or the 927th FR also at Kep. Finally, MiG-19Ss and MiG-17Fs of the 925th FR, based at Yen Bai, were occasionally encountered as well (*US Navy*)

commander of F-4 squadron VF-161 and on his sixth combat tour. Ruliffson saw a MiG-17 moving in on the A-6As as they made their Rockeye attacks, resisted the temptation to take it on and instead called in Houston's section. The A-6 flight left the target and headed out along a narrow valley, with the MiG in pursuit. Jerry Houston recalled;

'Kevin was about 95 per cent responsible for our getting that MiG. He'd reminded me about some armament switches I'd

Lt Cdr Jerry Houston and Lt(jg) Kevin Moore with the captain of *Coral Sea*, Capt Bill Harris, after their MiG kill mission. Jerry Houston assured the author that his sunglasses were worn to 'hide tears of joy'. VF-51 had become the first US Navy squadron to shoot down enemy aircraft in World War 2, Korea and Vietnam following its 26 June 1968 MiG-21 kill by Cdr 'Moose' Myers in an F-8H. VF-31 was the second. Houston and Moore were the first 'Screaming Eagles' crew to claim a MiG in the F-4 (*US Navy via Jerry B Houston*)

forgotten soon after coasting in and then he saw the 923rd FR MiG and coaxed me into a good kill position long before I had spotted it.'

'Devil' Houston saw the MiG's gunfire as it pursued the Intruders, two of which broke away to seek alternative egress routes, leaving the third A-6A with a MiG-17 closing on it.

Cdr Sheets then courageously moved in between the two adversaries, jinking his A-6A to avoid the MiG's 37 mm shells and drawing fire away from the other Intruder. He knew that the MiG's flight controls would have been ineffective at their 500-knot speed at just 100 ft about uneven karst terrain. Houston's radio had been modified to transmit the AIM-9's target-acquisition 'growl', so he was unable to warn Sheets that a Sidewinder launch was imminent.

'Sheets decided not to break away until he saw my missile fired – the ultimate decoy. It worked, but only because at the last minute (approaching minimum firing range and in total frustration) I decided to fire the missile, despite a chance that it could have locked on CAG's A-6. I didn't know he couldn't hear my frantic calls to "break and get the hell out of there". All he heard was the transmitted Sidewinder tone.'

Luckily, the A-6A was clear of danger and the AIM-9G wove its erratic course, finally entering the MiG's tailpipe and blowing off the rear half of the aircraft. Its pilot, Nguyen Van Bay, was killed. His wingman, Nguyen Van Luc, attacked Schroeder's Phantom II, but the latter evaded and Van Luc was ordered back to base.

A second attack on the same airfield target was ordered that afternoon, being allocated to *Kitty Hawk*'s CVW-11. Two VF-114 'Aardvarks' CAP sections were launched. The first was led by the squadron CO, Cdr John Pitzen (later posted missing in action after a 16 August hit by a SAM), who had to exchange his MiGCAP orbit for the BARCAP position flown by a section led by Lt Cdr Pete 'Viper' Pettigrew when his F-4J's radar went down. Pettigrew, a former Topgun instructor, had Lt Bob Hughes and Lt(jg) Joe Cruz as wingman in F-4J BuNo 157249. Pettigrew's RIO, Lt(jg) Mike McCabe, also had problems in getting any of his missiles to

VF-51 F-4B BuNo 153027 chained down to *Coral Sea*'s flightdeck during a port call in 1972. This aeroplane has been adorned with a MiG-17 silhouette even though it was not a MiG killer. 'Screaming Eagle 103' was assigned to Lt Cdr Jerry Houston, who had indeed downed a MiG earlier in the cruise. VF-51's famously colourful 'supersonic can-opener' unit decor for their somewhat battle-weary, ex-US Marine Corps F-4Bs originated when the CO, Cdr Tom Tucker, sent Ens John Letter on a corrosion control and aircraft painting course at NAS North Island. This was, as VF-51 pilot Jerry Houston explained, 'to determine which areas made the most sense to paint and ones that couldn't be painted on the F-4. He found out which panels came off most often during routine maintenance and then devised a squadron paint scheme to avoid them. Then there was a squadron competition for designing paint scheme proposals. Our supersonic eagle won hands down. The Miramar wags said all the design lacked was mud-flaps and a long raccoon tail on an aerial. This was especially true since most outfits were looking for ways to hide their airplanes. We didn't care. We were going hunting and prayed to be found' (*US Navy*)

tune and he had, in any case, launched with only two AIM-7E-2s and four AIM-9Gs.

'Red Crown' (Larry Nowell) warned of four MiG-21s coming in from the north, and Pettigrew's 'Linfield' section turned towards them. Cruz attained a radar contact at 25 miles, noting that the 'blue bandits' were in a V-formation so that they would look like two aircraft on radar. His jet became the 'shooter'. All four men saw distant aircraft at around four miles and closed for the necessary visual ID. They followed the MiGs around a single 360-degree turn inside a wide valley and Hughes fired an AIM-9G with a homing tone at 45 degrees 'angle off', but it picked up the target and blew parts of the tail off a MiG-21 flown by Le Van Lap, who managed to eject safely. Hughes then approached the third MiG-21, firing two AIM-9Gs, but this time neither of them homed successfully. Pettigrew, in 'Linfield 201' (BuNo 157245), drew in abeam Hughes' Phantom II and both pilots went after the lead MiG-21. Pettigrew fired first, followed moments later by Hughes with his final AIM-9G, and both missiles flew into the MiG's engine, shredding the aircraft and forcing the pilot to eject. Low on fuel, the two F-4Js returned to the carrier to help celebrate a day with three MiG shoot-downs.

On 8 May, as Nixon's Operation *Pocket Money* (the aerial mining campaign mounted by TF 77 against the harbours and ports of North Vietnam) was announced, the Cunningham and Driscoll team, again flying F-4J BuNo 157267, and with Brian Grant on their wing, downed their second MiG-17. The day's target, for which they were in a MiGCAP, was a large transport staging area near Dong Suong. As they set up their orbit over coastal waters, 'Red Crown' gave them a heading towards intermittent MiG contacts at a range of 60 miles. Brian 'Bulldog' Grant recalled;

'Unfortunately, the "Red Crown" control vectors seemed "spotty" to me, and sensing a set-up, I called the flight to make an in-place course reversal, which placed Randy Cunningham behind me in a position to down his second MiG, conveniently trapped at my "six o'clock". The trap that I had sensed was in fact realised when two other MiG-17s that had been trailing us flew directly over Randy's aircraft due to the course reversal.'

Cunningham saw the MiG that was firing at Grant's F-4J and advised him to jettison his centreline tank and 'bug out'.

Fortunately, the MiG pilot's 23 mm gunfire was (typically) inaccurate and Grant was able to evade an 'Atoll' missile that was also fired at him. As the MiG returned for another attempt Cunningham fired a Sidewinder considerably off axis to distract the VPAF pilot, and was then attacked by two more MiG-17s. One released an 'Atoll', which, with Driscoll's help, Cunningham avoided, and he continued to pursue the MiG that was still chasing Grant. He fired an AIM-9G that damaged the enemy aircraft's tail, and as Cunningham prepared to fire again the MiG suddenly caught fire and crashed into a hillside.

Meanwhile, his two pursuers moved outwards to his rear left and right, firing at him from 3000 ft, so that they could catch him whichever way he turned. It was up to Brian Grant to save his leader, who was now manoeuvring so hard that he over-stressed 'Showtime 112' with 10g contortions that damaged the flaps. Eventually, Cunningham entered cloud cover and flew towards the sun, hoping it would mask his afterburner heat from any further 'Atoll' shots. Brian Grant explains what happened next;

'I went to high cover and jettisoned my centreline fuel tank. Rolling in from a high perch caused the MiGs to disengage Randy, go for low cloud cover and escape. We followed in vain, then egressed to refuel. This was a classic mutual support textbook fight, as we had practised it.'

On their return to the 'boat', Cunningham, frustrated at losing a third MiG, shot an AIM-9G at an NVA supply truck and its infrared seeker homed successfully on the vehicle's hot engine. Their aerial victory caused elation aboard TF 77 ships.

May 1972 was a key month in the US Navy's air war, with 16 MiGs destroyed in 17 days. Two of the first three downed that month fell to VF-114 'Aardvarks' crews, who bagged a pair of MiG-21s. Naval Academy graduate and acknowledged expert pilot Lt Bob Hughes (left), with Californian Lt(jg) Joe Cruz (second left), flew F-4J BuNo 157249 'Linfield 206' when they downed their 'Fishbed' on 6 May. Topgun instructor Lt Cdr Pete 'Viper' Pettigrew (right) and Lt(jg) Mike McCabe (third from left) claimed their MiG-21 in the same engagement whilst flying BuNo 157245 'Linfield 201'. McCabe, who had only 100 hours in F-4s at the time of the encounter and had missed going through a fleet replacement squadron course on the jet prior to joining VF-51, later became a vice admiral. Their controller that day was Senior Radarman Larry 'Ace' Nowell, who was instrumental in the downing of 12 MiGs whilst providing fighter control from the 'Red Crown' ship *Chicago* (*US Navy*)

Lt Bob Hughes climbs into the cockpit of VF-114 F-4J BuNo 157248 'Linfield 214' on board *Kitty Hawk* during the early stages of CVW-11's 1972 WestPac. As previously noted, his MiG kill mission with Lt(jg) Joe Cruz was flown in 'Linfield 206'. Many of the manufacturer's copious stencil markings on US Navy Phantom IIs that are clearly in evidence here were not reinstated when the aircraft went for deep maintenance and refinishing at a naval depot (*US Navy*)

CHAPTER FOUR

PHANTOM II AS A FIGHTER

F-4J BuNo 155753 was assigned to VF-92 CO Cdr Philip J Scott during the unit's 1971-72 WestPac. Following a four-year association with VF-92 that only ended when the squadron disestablished in December 1975, this aircraft saw out its remaining nine years of frontline service with the US Marine Corps. Upgraded into an F-4S in the late 1970s, BuNo 155753 flew with VMFA-232 and VMFA-115 until sent to MASDC in June 1984. It was eventually scrapped in August 2008 (*US Navy*)

Operation *Freedom Train,* essentially aimed at stopping supply vehicles reaching the 'panhandle' area of South Vietnam, was a precursor to Operation *Linebacker I* (originally code-named *Rolling Thunder Alpha*), which drew together all the attack initiatives against North Vietnam. It began on 10 May with strikes north of the 20th parallel and continued until 23 October when it seemed that the Hanoi regime was ready for meaningful peace negotiations. The objective was to cut North Vietnam off from outside logistical support from its communist allies by land and sea. At the same time Nixon went to Moscow in an attempt to improve relations, and he also visited China in February 1972, playing the two countries off against each other and reducing Chinese support for North Vietnam.

Restrictions on bombing many of the military sites that US pilots had seen for many years as priority targets were at last lifted after the Spring Invasion showed the continued hollowness of the Paris peace talks. President Nixon brought a new approach to the use of his military resources. In his words, 'We have the power to destroy his war-making capacity. The only question is whether we have the will to use that power. What distinguishes me from [President] Johnson is that I have the will in spades'.

However, the relatively small numbers of US tactical aircraft in the region meant that large-scale attacks on North Vietnam had to wait until reinforcements could arrive in the form of additional carriers for TF 77 and USAF fighter wings at bases in Thailand. The air power that was already available in-theatre was immediately used to provide close support for ARVN regiments as the massive invasion force continued to push south. It succeeded in blunting the invasion by denying insurgent forces in South Vietnam the 1000 tons of supplies they required each day to sustain their incursion.

During *Linebacker I* US Navy strikes accounted for twice the number of sorties as the USAF effort, and F-4s, A-6s (the principal night-attackers until USAF F-111As returned to Thailand in September 1972) and A-7s destroyed 185 bridges – almost double the USAF total – with conventional munitions. Carriers launched their attack squadrons in Alpha strikes by day and again on night reconnaissance sorties loaded with bombs and flares. They also claimed more than 500 railway trucks, 666 road vehicles and almost 1000 barges and supply boats destroyed. Disruption of the network in this way meant that large supply dumps accumulated at breaks in the routes, making attractive targets for tactical air strikes. As the campaign moved deeper into the Hanoi/Haiphong heartland, US Navy strike packages accounted for up to 85 per cent of the missions, and in August the naval sortie rate peaked at 4750 from the five carriers that were on station.

The US Navy's first major action in May 1972 was Operation *Pocket Money*, ordered by President Nixon to commence on the 9th despite earlier fears of exacerbating friction with Russia and China. Mining the harbours and ports of North Vietnam had been suggested by Adm U S Grant Sharp, Commander-in-Chief, US Pacific Command, near the beginning of the war, but it had been ruled out as a threat to the shipping from many nations that regularly delivered war supplies to North Vietnam.

On 9 May six of CVW-15's A-7Es from VA-94 and VA-22, led by Cdr Len Giuliani (CO of the latter unit), and three A-6As from VMA(AW)-224, with CAG Cdr Roger 'Blinky' Sheets in the lead, delivered their 36 1000-lb Mk 52 Mod 2/3 parachute-retarded magnetic mines and 500-lb Mk 36 Mod 2 Destructor acoustic mines. These were dropped at altitudes below 500 ft into the approach to Haiphong harbour, through which 85 per cent of North Vietnam's supplies arrived from around the world.

Phantom IIs from *Coral Sea* were on station to protect the A-6 and A-7 bombers, which were subjected to intense AAA during the mission. However, the proximity of the operation to coastal defences required the force's main air defence to be provided by Talos missiles, 31 ft in length. They had a 65-mile range and were installed on the cruisers *Long Beach* and *Chicago*, which were given a free-fire zone to engage any MiGs that might intervene. One MiG-21 awaiting GCI instructions to intercept the mining aircraft was shot down by a Talos at a range of 48 miles. Thanks

VF-111's F-4Bs on board *Coral Sea* were on hand to protect the aerial mining force during Operation *Pocket Money* in May 1972. Here, having just returned from such an escort mission for CVW-15's two A-7E units charged with sowing the minefields, 'Old Nick 203' (BuNo 151459) is towed past a fire suppression squad on deck, training for one of the most serious threats to a carrier, a major on-board fire. This aircraft was VF-111's second 'Old Nick 203' on its 1971-72 WestPac, as the original example (BuNo 150418) had been downed by an SA-2 on 30 December 1971 and its crew captured (*US Navy*)

to the employment of the Talos missile, the Phantom II units were spared from exposure to the ten SA-2 sites around Haiphong and from heavy AAA – US Navy attack aircraft were fired at by both, and it is likely that the damage inflicted on two Soviet cargo vessels off Haiphong was caused by misdirected AAA shells. After the mines were activated 72 hours later, no ships were able to enter or leave Haiphong for the rest of the year – and the main port was closed for 300 days.

Kitty Hawk's air group launched a 17-aircraft, early morning strike on the Nam Dinh rail complex as a diversionary raid on 9 May, although the strike package actually had to divert to two secondary targets. In the following eight months thousands more mines were laid in other ports and river estuaries. As a result, far more traffic was forced onto the railways and trails network, where it could be hit by tactical aircraft. Ammunition shortages caused by the mining of the harbours meant that the NVA's coastal defence gun batteries had exhausted their supply of shells by mid-May.

BATTLE COMMENCES

On 10 May joint USAF/US Navy attacks on highways and bridges began. More than 400 bridges were hit, including the massive, heavily defended, Paul Doumer (Long Bien) and Thanh Hoa bridges that had been frequently targeted but never destroyed during *Rolling Thunder*. USAF 8th TFW F-4s using *Pave Knife* laser targeting pods and *Paveway* precision-guided bombs took out or damaged many of the major road and rail bridges. The Doumer Bridge was a particularly valuable target, as all rail traffic from China or the port of Haiphong used it to reach central distribution points in Hanoi.

Following the bridge attacks, US Navy aircraft flew 294 sorties against targets in North Vietnam from *Coral Sea*, *Kitty Hawk* and *Constellation* that day, compared with 120 by USAF aircraft, of which 32 were made by F-4s configured as bombers. Substantial damage to railway yards in Haiphong and Hai Duong and storage and petroleum tank complexes at Cam Pha and Quan Bak was caused by Alpha strikes.

Eleven MiGs were shot down on the 10th, with eight of them being credited to US Navy crews, for the loss of two USAF F-4s to gunfire from Shenyang J-6s (Chinese-built MiG-19s) of the 925th FR, based at Yen Bai. Three of the successful US Navy Phantom II crews had experienced Topgun, and the overall success rate began to equate to the Korean War ratio. It was at least a major, if temporary, advance on the overall two-to-one advantage claimed by US pilots during *Rolling Thunder*, and on the overall loss rate between 1970 and 1973, when 28 American aircraft were lost to MiGs, only four of them from US Navy squadrons. As Seventh Air Force commander, and World War 2 ace, Gen John W Vogt commented in 1972;

'By July 1972, in the middle of the *Linebacker* operations, for the first time in the history of the USAF the loss-to-victory ratio swung in favour of the enemy. We were losing more aeroplanes than we were shooting down. This had never happened before anywhere in the world.'

He blamed this on 'going blind into a heavily netted threat radar environment, and confronting the best MiGs that the Soviets had available for export'. In fact, seven losses (all F-4s) to MiGs were recorded for July 1972, six of them from USAF units, in return for six MiGs (all 'Fishbeds') – a small and temporary margin, but an important disparity psychologically.

The outcome on 10 May was quite different. *Constellation*'s 33-aircraft strike force was the first to set off for its target, followed at ten-minute intervals by similar formations from *Kitty Hawk* and *Coral Sea*, and observed by the North

Vietnamese early warning radars and the ubiquitous Soviet spy ship *Kursograf* for most of their journey. As each aerial armada approached Haiphong, its two MiGCAP F-4 flights, each with four Phantom IIs, moved to orbits around the city, ready to intercept incoming MiG opposition. A four-strong F-4 flak suppression flight immediately preceded the strike flights, dropping six Mk 20 Rockeye canisters from each aircraft to reduce the AAA aimed at the attackers. Two A-7E *Iron Hand* flights responded to 'Fan Song' radars with Shrike missiles, forcing them to shut down and hopefully break lock on any SA-2s that were already launched, while EKA-3Bs provided jamming and aerial tanking. The main strike force included six A-6As and ten A-7s, while an RA-5C with a single F-4 escort launched to collect bomb damage assessment (BDA) information.

A-6As delivered the first ordnance and evaded numerous radar and optically guided SA-2s. One SAM was aimed at an F-4 MiGCAP orbiting to the south of the target, but a Shrike closed the radar down and the SAM ceased to track the Phantom II, exploding far away. For many F-4 and A-6 crews sent on SAM and flak suppression missions, there was the inescapable sense that they were there to force the enemy to use up his stocks of missiles and ammunition while they tried to dodge the barrage and deliver their own ordnance.

Alpha strikes targeted Hai Duong's petroleum storage and railway marshalling area, as well as the military port facilities at Cam Pha and Hon Gai, causing some damage to a Soviet cargo vessel at the latter site. Strikes were monitored by the PIRAZ cruiser *Chicago* and a range of electronic surveillance aircraft including USAF EC-121Ds and RC-135Ms and the US Navy's EP-3B Orions and E-2B Hawkeyes. The last of *Constellation*'s Phantom IIs over the target was the single VF-92 escort for the post-strike RA-5C, crossing Haiphong at 600 knots at 4000 ft and attracting plenty of AAA and two SA-2s, one of which exploded close to the F-4. The fighter was inverted by the blast, but pilot Lt Olsen recovered it and escaped. The second SA-2 detonated close to the RVAH-11 Vigilante, causing superficial damage.

VF-92 squadron members line up in their 'Friday flightsuits' in front of their 'CAG bird' F-4J, assigned to CVW-9 CO Cdr Gus Eggert, during the historic 1972 WestPac. Thirty aircrew officers on strength for VF-92 were supported by 245 enlisted men during a typical Vietnam combat cruise. On board ship, F-4 crews had staterooms that were shared between at least eight officers, who graduated to four-man rooms if they did a second tour. The CO and XO had their own staterooms, although conditions were still very basic due to inadequate air conditioning and periods during the day when the steam demands of the catapults reduced the amount of water for drinking or showers on some carriers. A tour with a squadron usually lasted two-and-a-half years, and during this time a pilot or RIO could be expected to complete two combat deployments of around eight months each (*Author's collection*)

Lt Austin 'Hawk' Hawkins (with helmet removed for a more flattering photograph) and RIO Lt Jerry Hill formate with Lt Curt Dosé in 'Silver Kite 212' (BuNo 155797), which is fully armed with missiles for a CAP mission. This was the aircraft in which Cdr Harry Blackburn and Lt Steve Rudloff were shot down on 10 May 1972 (*Author's collection via Curt Dosé*)

F-4J BuNo 155813 'Silver Kite 210' was flown by Lt 'Hawk' Hawkins and Lt(jg) Jay Tinker on their MiG-baiting mission over Kep airfield during which three of their AIM-9s narrowly missed their MiG-21 target. This aircraft subsequently served with the US Marine Corps – both before and after it was upgraded to F-4S specification – until it was destroyed in a fatal take-off crash at MCAS Yuma, Arizona, on 11 December 1984 (*Author's collection*)

The northern TARCAP for *Constellation*'s target area was manned by VF-92 and led by Lt Austin Hawkins and Lt(jg) Jay Tinker, with Lt Curt 'Dozo' Dosé and Lt Cdr Jim 'Routeslip' McDevitt in F-4J BuNo 157269 'Silver Kite 211'. Curt Dosé recalled;

'Our first strike MiGCAP was unique in that the strike was close to the coast, so the strike aircraft were quickly on and off the target, then "feet wet". We still had lots of gas when the "blue bandits" [MiG-21] guard frequency calls came from threats to the north. Our initial turn to intercept these threats was proper and expected. It was partly coincidence that we ended up heading right for Kep [airfield].'

Although moving away from their strike orbit could have been construed as deliberate MiG hunting, rather than reacting to an immediate threat to the Alpha aircraft, Dosé had already supposed that giving them a target close to the major MiG airfields near Hanoi was an invitation for aerial combat. However, their time over Kep, below 'Red Crown' radar coverage, was a source of concern. In a letter home (written whilst strapped into the cockpit of an Alert Five F-4J) anticipating their 8 May Son Toi shipment

area strike, Dosé had conjectured that 'the MiGs are really the primary objective, and not the 500 trucks'.

The next letter home to Jacksonville, written in haste after the 10 May morning strike, began;

'Wahoo! Scratch one! I'm going back to Haiphong this afternoon, but I bagged one MiG and damaged another this morning over Kep airfield. It is VF-92's first MiG kill and it was beautiful! Over the airfield at 5000 ft, we saw the MiG-17s in revetments, then two MiG-21s holding short of the northern end and *then* two MiG-21s taking off in the opposite direction. We went into 'burner and pulled around, coming down the runway at about 1000 ft and 600 knots, pulling up and left at about 500 knots. We caught the MiGs about three miles off the runway at 500 ft. I fired a 'winder at the right one [flown by Nguyen Van Ngai, who died in the subsequent crash], which went off under him and I fired again. The 'winder flew right up his tailpipe and exploded.

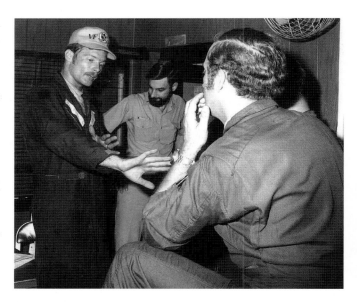

'I then pulled on to the left MiG and fired again. The missile just missed (about ten degrees behind him). My last 'winder did not come off the rail. Hawkins fired three 'winders at the second MiG also [flown by seven-victory ace Dang Ngoc Ngu of the 921st FR, who would later be killed when he was shot down by a USAF F-4E] while I was shooting, but they were close misses. Two more MiG-21s jumped us, and we left the area out of missiles, with "Atolls" going off around us.'

At least two of the AIM-9Gs belonging to the 'Silver Kings' struck objects on the ground since the fight had taken place at such low altitude.

Jim McDevitt had noticed the 'gleaming silver finish' of the MiG-21MFs on the runway as they crossed it at very low altitude, and Curt Dosé judged that they had 'pure red stars – Russian, not North Vietnamese markings. My best guess is that they had just been delivered. We were the first ones to face the new MiG-21MF with low-altitude supersonic capability – quite a surprise to us, – and almost a fatal one for Hawkins and Tinker'. One of the MiG-21MFs followed them, gaining on the F-4 as they made for the coast. At a range of less than a mile, it fired an 'Atoll' at Hawkins' jet, which the Phantom II pilot narrowly avoided by making an in-place turn.

Dosé had used the 'loose deuce' formation tactics well in watching Hawkins' tail and warning him to turn hard. 'We quickly adjusted to the new observed speed of the MF', he explained. 'It became even more important to get rid of the F-4's centreline drop tank in a low-altitude fight. This was difficult because it had to be dropped below a certain speed [500 knots, wings level and in a positive 1g situation, with the tank either empty or full, or else it could depart at an angle and damage the aircraft] that went by very fast when getting aggressive in a developing situation.

10 May 1972 was an historic day for carrier-based Phantom II squadrons, with eight MiGs destroyed and the creation of the US Navy's first ace crew in the form of Lt Randy Cunningham and Lt(jg) Willie Driscoll. Among the victors were former instructor Lt Curt 'Dozo' Dosé (seen here at left in discussion with Lt Cdr Gordon Williamson) and his RIO, ex-Skywarrior bombardier/navigator Lt Cdr Jim 'Routeslip' McDevitt. Lt Dosé's father was a World War 2 F6F Hellcat pilot who had shot down two Mitsubishi A6M Zero-sens. Dosé had attended Topgun and embarked on his second war cruise with VF-92 determined to get a MiG. On 10 May he and McDevitt scored the squadron's one and only MiG kill whilst in a supersonic dive in the direction of the runway at Kep airfield. The VPAF pilot, who did not survive, was initially thought to have been a Soviet instructor (known to the US Navy as 'Top Gunsky'), although VPAF records list him as Nguyen Van Ngai of the 921st FR (*US Navy*)

Lt Curt Dosé's self-portrait includes a reflection of the instrument panel of his 'Silver Kings' F-4J (*Author's collection via Curt Dosé*)

If you dropped faster than the limit it could take your horizontal tail off – not desirable over enemy territory'.

Dosé surmised, as did many of his colleagues, that the MiGs might have been flown by Soviet pilots – a suggestion that was energetically denied by the North Vietnamese. His section's decision to go 'coincidentally MiG hunting' had consequences for the day's second Alpha strike, for CVW-9's CO, Cdr Gus Eggert, felt obliged to issue an order banning his F-4 crews from 'trolling for MiGs'.

That second strike brought bad news for the 'Silver Kings' when their XO, Cdr Harry Lee 'Habu' Blackburn and his RIO, Lt Steve 'Sar' Rudloff, in 'Silver Kite 212' (BuNo 155797), were hit by AAA on a TARCAP over the Hai Duong railyard target, although North Vietnamese records credit the aircraft's destruction to future six-victory MiG-21 ace Le Thanh Dao of the 927th FR. They had obeyed orders and stayed close to the two 'Pouncer' *Iron Hand* A-7s that they were escorting. 'Silver Kite 207' (BuNo unknown), flown by wingman Lt Rod 'Dilly' Dilworth, with Lt(jg) Jerry Hill as RIO, was also hit and lost its starboard engine, but Dilworth was able to stay long enough to see Blackburn and his RIO land by parachute. He then nursed his F-4J out of the fight, streaming fuel from numerous holes in its fuselage as he jettisoned its missiles before returning to *Constellation*, with a glowing fire-warning light, to make a textbook single-engine landing. 'Silver Kite 207' never flew again.

Rudloff, on his 295th combat mission and third tour of duty, had recommended to Blackburn that they should remain on station after the strikers departed, leaving coverage of their exit to the flak suppression F-4Js, which had already delivered their Rockeyes. He had made several radar contacts and hoped that he might catch a MiG. On their second orbit Rudloff saw a 'wall of flak. I knew we were going to get hit. They had us zeroed in. It looked to me like barrage fire'.

When the 85 mm shell exploded in their tail area, the Phantom II immediately began to blaze and Rudloff was temporarily blinded by an electrical explosion in his cockpit. He called for ejection and drifted down on his parachute, conscious of bullets from ground fire hitting his parachute canopy and watched by 'Willie' Driscoll in 'Showtime 100'. Still blinded, Rudloff hit the ground hard, injuring his right ankle. He tried to signal to a passing aircraft (Lt Cdr Mike Gravely in an *Iron Hand* A-7E) that he was alive. 'I collapsed back down again, so I don't know if that pilot ever saw me stand up so that he could report that I was alive. I do know that Harry [Blackburn] and I were declared "presumed captured". Harry was in the cell next to mine in Hai Duong [PoW prison] being severely beaten that afternoon, and I believe that's when he died'. Steve Rudloff remained in his cell until March 1973, but Blackburn's fate remained a mystery, as the North Vietnamese denied knowledge of his capture.

VF-96's Lts Matt Connelly and Tom Blonski, in 'Showtime 106' (BuNo 155769), and his wingman Lt Aaron R Campbell, in 'Showtime 113' (BuNo 157296), were also over Hai Duong in a TARCAP at 18,000 ft when Matt noticed the lack of SAMs opposing the strike. VPAF controllers were vectoring a large number of MiGs into the area, unnoticed by 'Red Crown' radar. As Curt Dosé noted in a letter, this was 'the first time the MiGs came in force to repel a strike. As the strike aircraft started exiting the area, they were hit by at least 15 MiG-17s and four MiG-21s. I've always dreaded that possibility, thinking that we would lose several A-7s and A-6s, but they were fantastic. They were yelling like plucked chickens and swerving around a bit aimlessly, but they kept the MiGs off long enough for the F-4s to help them'.

RIO Lt Cdr Jim McDevitt (left), a former A-3 bombardier/navigator, and Lt Curt Dosé (right) pose with their plane captain and 'Silver Kite 211' (BuNo 157269) in which they shot down a MiG-21 on 10 May 1972 (*Author's collection via Curt Dosé*)

Dosé saw an A-7E being chased by two MiG-17s and started to set up Sparrows as he dived to intervene. The F-4J's radar failed at that point and he reverted to a 'heat' missile, firing at the edge of the AIM-9G's performance envelope. Like other pilots that day, he found that the fight was at too close quarters to use AIM-7s. Dosé's opponent performed a typically tight 180-degree turn back into the F-4s, almost colliding with Campbell's Phantom II and hastening his departure from the fight.

Connelly then climbed to meet MiG-17s circling above him, chasing one that also turned tightly but then reversed its turn, allowing a Sidewinder opportunity. On his combat tape, which also recorded transmissions from Cunningham and Driscoll's triple kill at the same time, Connelly can be heard saying 'Splash one' as his AIM-9G hit the MiG at 1000 ft and the enemy fighter exploded. While Cunningham was in pursuit of another MiG-17 nearby, Connelly went after a second target. 'The second MiG kill was a random aircraft simply flying by', he later recalled. 'I turned in pursuit. He saw me and attempted to break with me, but lost sight after two reversals. He rolled wings level and I fired a Sidewinder to a near miss. The missile exploded on proximity fuse and cut off the whole tail assembly of the MiG-17 with its expanding rod warhead. As I flew past the unflyable MiG the pilot ejected, allowing me to watch the full ejection sequence. I was surprised to see that their parachute canopies were square in shape'.

Connelly had just claimed the 923rd FR flight leader, Nguyen Van Tho, who, although now floating down beneath a fully deployed parachute, was not yet out of danger. Cunningham's aircraft, heading out after scoring one more MiG than Connelly, came perilously close to running into him as he descended.

In another simultaneous dogfight, Lt Steve Shoemaker and Lt(jg) Keith 'Cannonball' Crenshaw were charging through the six minutes long melée for

At the top of this photograph is F-4J BuNo 157267, flown by VF-96's Lt Cunningham and Lt(jg) Driscoll for their MiG kills on 19 January and 8 May 1972. In the foreground is F-4J BuNo 155800, which they used for their epic triple MiG haul – claimed over a period of just eight minutes – on 10 May 1972. The aircraft was shot down by an SA-2 shortly after the last of the 'Fresco-Cs' had been destroyed. BuNo 157267, by contrast, has been an exhibit in the San Diego Aerospace Museum for almost 30 years (*US Navy*)

a third time, having successfully used an AIM-9G inside minimum range to frighten a MiG-17 off Lt Dave Erickson's 'Showtime 102' (BuNo 15580) as he in turn protected the F-4J of his XO, Cdr Dwight D Timm. A former *Blue Angel* who was on his third tour, 'Shoeman' Shoemaker, flying 'Showtime 111' (BuNo 155749), had been tasked with escorting Lt Cdr Gravely's *Iron Hand* A-7E. Shoemaker had almost hit Brian Grant's F-4J, which was also heading for the MiG that threatened Erickson. Grant went for another target, but his missile appeared to home onto the sun instead.

As the Alpha strike jets headed out to sea, Shoemaker spotted a MiG-17 trailing F-4J 'Showtime 100' (BuNo 155800) and sent Cunningham a warning. The MiG pilot noticed Shoemaker and turned to escape him, but 'Shoeman' dived to around 1000 ft and got behind the VPAF jet. He launched an AIM-9G from 2000 ft as the MiG entered a turning fight with him. He then broke away to check that he was not being followed. As he did so, Crenshaw saw a pall of smoke on the ground and neither crewman could see the MiG anywhere. They were later credited with a kill, but immediately had to deal with another threat from a MiG-17 that appeared beside them and started to acquire a firing position. Shoemaker lit up the afterburners, left the enemy standing and headed out.

Connelly and Blonski then came very close to equalling Cunningham's score for the day, ironically by driving another MiG-17 off his tail. 'Showtime 100', damaged by a SAM, had no afterburner and the MiG was closing on it as Connelly radioed another warning and, still without a radar, launched a Sparrow in boresight mode, which scared the MiG off. Seconds later the radar began to work and the crew attempted to locate the MiG for a real Sparrow attack, but it had vanished, so they had to head for the water in afterburner. En route, they were able to warn 'Showtime 100' of a MiG-21 and two more MiG-17s that posed threats, enabling Cunningham to evade them as he coaxed his battered Phantom II on the last few miles of its career. Connelly landed on board *Constellation* with only 500 lb of fuel remaining.

FIVE DOWN

Cunningham and Driscoll's 10 May was a day of fortuitous events and tests of skill, beginning with their late addition to the flak suppression flight for *Constellation*'s afternoon Alpha strike. Their Phantom II was loaded with six Mk 20 Rockeye canisters, two AIM-7s and four AIM-9s. As they orbited above the strikers, they saw Blackburn's aircraft hit by

AAA. The Hai Duong target had been effectively wiped out by the previous Alphas, so they were directed to a secondary objective near the railway yards. Cunningham and Grant rolled in together to drop their ordnance, but seeing their target disappear in a cloud of smoke from the A-7Es' 1000-lb bombs, they adjusted their aim, avoided two unguided SA-2s and hit a large storage building instead.

At that point about 20 enemy fighters appeared, and Brian Grant warned 'Showtime 100' that two MiG-17s were on their tail and shooting big 37 mm rounds at them. Cunningham made a quick reversal into one of them, which shot past, and he calculated that the VPAF pilot would be having trouble operating his controls at such a high speed. While Grant dealt with the second MiG, Cunningham released an AIM-9 from 1000 ft and blew his adversary to pieces.

Cunningham then tried to 'drag out' the other MiG for Grant, who had two more MiG-17s on his tail and was unable to take the chance of a likely kill, as he explained. 'Approaching the MiGs threatening Randy, my RIO reported that a MiG was firing guns at us. We disengaged, did defensive manoeuvres and evaded the MiGs to rejoin the fight in progress'. The two Phantom IIs made steep vertical climbs to 15,000 ft and blew off their centreline tanks. As they did so, Cunningham witnessed Matt Connelly's MiG exploding, and saw a defensive 'wagon wheel' circle of eight more 'Fresco-Cs' below him at 10,000 ft. This time-honoured tactic was intended to draw unsuspecting US fighters in to pursue a MiG, and then be attacked by the following VPAF jet in the orbit.

Two F-4s had already joined the circus, making themselves vulnerable by slowing to 350 knots in the process. One was 'Showtime 112' (BuNo 157267), flown by VF-96 CO Cdr Dwight Timm and his RIO, Lt Jim Fox. As it hurtled out of the 'wagon wheel', the jet almost hit Cunningham's F-4. Timm had a MiG-17 close behind him, a MiG-21 further back and another MiG-17 turning with him, but hidden below his aircraft. He was also in afterburner, preventing Cunningham from firing a 'Fox Two' Sidewinder as he moved in behind the VPAF pursuers. Cunningham called for Timm to reverse his turn and force the closest MiG clear of his underside so that 'Showtime 100' could pick it off, but Timm kept going, assuming that Cunningham was referring to the MiGs behind him rather than the real threat on his underside.

Meanwhile, 'Willie' Driscoll noticed four more MiG-17s gradually catching up with their F-4J, and then detected the silvery glint of a further two MiGs diving on them from high above. At this point Cunningham thought 'There can't be any more MiG-17s in the world', and seconds later he realised that the new threat was a pair of supersonic MiG-19s. They began to fire, and he turned sharply to force them away behind him, before

The 10 May 1972 triple MiG kills by Lt Randall 'Duke' Cunningham and Lt(jg) William 'Irish' Driscoll – confirming them as the only US Navy aces of the Vietnam War – were taken as final proof of the value of Topgun. Although Cunningham was temporarily assigned to the course, rather than completing it as a student, he studied and absorbed its lessons avidly. Driscoll also attributed their success to good 'team chemistry'. In 2017, with Bill Freckleton and Garry Weigand, they met up with some of the MiG pilots with whom they had duelled so fiercely over North Vietnam (*US Navy*)

returning to Timm's MiG-17. Maintaining 550 knots so as to keep the other MiG-17s at bay behind him, Cunningham had to accelerate on several occasions when Driscoll warned him of gunfire from the MiG-17 pack. Cdr Timm finally broke away from the 'belly hugging' MiG-17, allowing Cunningham a clear shot – his AIM-9 disintegrated the VPAF fighter.

The strike force had by then left the area and Cunningham realised that it was time to go, although he had become separated from Grant's F-4. As he headed out, yet another MiG approached them from ahead at their 'two o'clock' position. Cunningham decided to head straight at him in order to make his task of turning back onto their tail as hard as possible. However, the MiG pilot opened up with short bursts of 23 mm cannon fire. Cunningham resorted to the basic Topgun tactic of 'going vertical', which would usually leave a MiG-17 behind, but the MiG pilot followed him upwards, canopy to canopy. Cunningham accelerated in afterburner, leaving the MiG some distance behind but in a good position to shoot at him.

Diving to escape this unusually daring pilot, whose identity remains unconfirmed (Do Hang and Tra Van Kiem were the two 923rd FR pilots who apparently died in conflicts with 'Showtime 100' that day), Cunningham waited for the MiG to follow and then climbed into him, hoping to roll in behind him for a Sidewinder shot. The MiG pilot thought otherwise and the fight degenerated into a series of 'rolling scissors' manoeuvres that slowed the F-4J to around 200 knots. Using his superior turning circle, the VPAF pilot matched every one of Cunningham's moves, forcing him to run and regain a speed of 600 knots, before going vertical once again in a 60-degree vertical turn, followed by a repeat of the scissors manoeuvre. A third climb allowed Cunningham to reach a point where he could reverse down towards the oncoming MiG, but this time he used his last-ditch tactic of chopping the throttles to idle and extending his speed brakes. Controlling the aircraft with the rudder as its speed dropped to 150 knots in full afterburner, he saw the MiG shoot out in front of him for the first time and then momentarily stall as it attempted to match Cunningham's roll. The VPAF pilot pitched over into a dive as if to leave the fight, and Cunningham was able to move in behind him. Despite being aimed at a target with a background of heat-reflecting terrain, his AIM-9 found the MiG's tailpipe and black smoke emerged after the fighter was hit. Moments later the MiG crashed from a 45-degree dive without an attempted ejection.

Although this fifth MiG had made them the first American air aces of the war, Cunningham and Driscoll still had more challenges to face that day. As they made for the coast, Connolly chased off another MiG-17 in hot pursuit of their F-4 (Cunningham reckoned there were actually four enemy fighters behind them), and he judged that the MiG's gunfire caused damage that eventually felled 'Showtime 100'. 'The MiG definitely had

F-4J 155800 'Showtime 100' bombing, straight and level, as part of a VF-96 flight in the early spring of 1972. On radar-directed bombing missions above cloud, SAMs were the major threat. F-4 crews could out-manoeuvre an SA-2 if they had enough visual warning of its approach, but if the missiles were fired through a thick cloud-base or in salvoes, as they often were, the F-4 could rapidly run out of energy in its attempts to avoid them, or be forced down to an altitude where AAA was a greater threat. Here, each of these jets is armed with AIM-7E-2 missiles in the rear Sparrow wells and AIM-9Gs on the inner wing pylons (*US Navy*)

a firing solution on Randy, who was wings level, in basic engine, climbing out of the engagement airspace. I feel this MiG did enough damage to his F-4 either to cripple its ECM capabilities [denying him SAM warnings] or actually cause it to subsequently become unflyable'.

Seconds later, Driscoll alerted his pilot to a MiG-21 and yet another MiG-17 approaching head-on. They also passed close to heavy 85 mm flak bursts and two SA-2s that zoomed past them. The two enemy fighters flashed past at close range but there was worse to come. As they overflew Nam Dinh, another SA-2 exploded close enough to them for Driscoll to hear shrapnel hitting the Phantom II's fuselage. The jet quickly caught fire and both main hydraulic systems began to drain out, causing the stabilator to lock and forcing the aircraft into a nose-up attitude. Cunningham remembered that it was possible to keep an F-4 flying for a while without hydraulics by using full rudder to make the aircraft yaw and bring the nose down again, with speed brakes extended, when it seemed that a steep dive was imminent. He duly coaxed 'Showtime 100' onwards for another 20 crucial miles over land in this way with alternate rudder, speed brakes and afterburner as the fire worsened.

Luckily all the MiGs had gone home by then, but following two internal explosions the rolling motions became too severe to control as the rudder had by then lost all hydraulic power. Suddenly, the crippled Phantom II stalled and entered a spin. The resourceful Cunningham released the landing parachute to try and stabilise the aircraft and squeeze out a few more miles, as they were still over the coastline. Surrounded by the crews of A-7Es and other F-4Js yelling at them to get out of the tumbling Phantom II, they ejected and landed in the muddy waters at the mouth of the Red River. A flotilla of North Vietnamese boats headed out to capture them, but they were beaten off by the F-4s and A-7s, allowing an HH-3A helicopter from HC-7 Det 110, embarked in USS *Okinawa* (LPH-3) to pick them up. Matt Connelly, from another VF-96 CAP, watched 'Showtime 100' spinning down in flames about five miles out to sea.

Coral Sea's VF-51, escorting a separate strike at Cam Pha (together with *Kitty Hawk*'s air wing) claimed the eighth, and final, US Navy kill on that momentous day from an offshore MiGCAP 20 miles south of Hanoi. Lt Cdr Chuck Schroeder and Lt(jg) Dale Arends, with Lt Ken 'Ragin' Cajun' Cannon and Lt Bud Morris (the squadron's RIO training officer) as wingmen in 'Screaming Eagle 111' (BuNo 151398), were vectored past the

Battle-weary F-4B BuNo 151398 assigned to Lt Winston 'Mad Dog' Copeland and Lt(jg) Dale Arends and flown by Lts Ken 'Ragin Cajun' Cannon and Bud Morris as 'Screaming Eagle 111' on 10 May 1972. Cannon was a former Crusader pilot who joined VF-51 in 1971, while Bud Morris had completed two previous tours with VF-154 prior to taking charge of training for VF-51's 'back-seaters'. A single AIM-9 was used for their MiG-17 kill. Upgraded into an F-4N following this deployment and then passed on to Japan-based VF-161 in the summer of 1973, this aircraft was placed in storage at MASDC in July 1977 and sold for scrapping in April 1990 (*Author's collection*) large-scale air battle over Hai Duong and descended to low altitude, where they saw a lone MiG-17 heading north at 2000 ft. Schroeder moved in behind the 'red bandit', which performed a barrel roll that put it behind his Phantom II and made him accelerate away. The MiG pilot apparently lost sight of the F-4B flown by Cannon and Morris, however, and they gained a firing position behind it, releasing an AIM-9 that severed the MiG's tail section. The Phantom II had to fly through a cloud of MiG debris as the VPAF fighter dived straight into the ground, with no ejection attempt seen.

Shortly thereafter *Constellation*'s CVW-9 flew its third Alpha strike of the day, which brought some tense moments for the crews involved, although the defences were generally lighter. Curt Dosé's *Iron Hand* escort F-4J had a lucky escape when two SA-2s followed his strenuous evasive manoeuvres but eventually passed very close to the aircraft without exploding. Another F-4J flown by Lts John Anderson and Les Roy had a similar escape, and the MiGs avoided engaging.

MIDWAY's MiGs

Midway's first line period in its third wartime cruise began on 30 April 1972 after the vessel had been diverted from CVW-5's carrier qualification period on 6 April, two months earlier than expected. F-4Bs were hastily mustered, including BuNo 153056 that was recovered from maintenance with an unreliable undercarriage. The air wing's two Phantom II units, VF-151 and VF-161, continued the successes against the VPAF that were the principal feature of F-4 operations in May. For these two units, their 205 days of combat operations set the record for any US Navy Phantom II squadrons during the conflict, and for VF-161, which completed 2322 sorties, it brought five MiG victories. They also had the unusual experience, for US Navy F-4 crews, of flying attack missions against visible ground forces with armoured vehicles and artillery during the battle of An Loc (which raged from 13 April to 20 July 1972), rather than dumping ordnance on unseen targets under jungle cover.

Like VF-96, VF-161 'Chargers' was manned by a number of very close pilot/RIO teams including Lt Cdr Ron 'Mugs' McKeown, who always described himself as the world's greatest fighter pilot, and his long-time back-seater, Lt Jack Ensch. McKeown had flown with VX-4, tested MiG-17s and MiG-21s at Groom Lake and composed an ACM training programme for VF-161 in 1970. He encouraged an intensely competitive ethos, and under the unit's new boss (Cdr Deacon Connell) for the 1971 cruise, VF-161 won the coveted Adm Joseph C Clifton Trophy for 'meritorious achievement by a fighter squadron while deployed aboard a carrier'. On 23 May 1972, a day when six MiGs were shot down, McKeown had a chance

F-4B (possibly BuNo 152243) 'Rock River 101' of the 'Chargers' roars away from *Midway* during *Linebacker* operations. VF-161 flew Phantom IIs for 22 years after conversion from the F-3B Demon in 1964 (it was last Pacific Fleet squadron to fly this earlier McDonnell fighter), making its first cruise from *Coral Sea* in 1965 and conducting the last ever F-4 cruise, on board *Midway*, in 1986. During six combat deployments crews from VF-161 downed six MiGs, including the only two US victories against MiG-19s as well as the very last aerial kill of the war on 12 January 1973 (*US Navy*) to prove his tactics, and the outcome was a double MiG kill in a fight with five enemy fighters, the award of a Navy Cross and the prospect of becoming the commanding officer of Topgun.

McKeown's F-4B, 'Rock River 100' (BuNo 153020), led a MiGCAP with Lt Mike Rabb and Lt(jg) Ken Crandall ('Rock River 112') for an Alpha strike on a Haiphong target. As they orbited between Haiphong and Kep airfield, they received notice of MiGs at 38 miles range and low altitude. The F-4B's radar gave them indistinct returns at around 3500 ft and they kept a close watch ahead, hoping to spot the target aircraft. Crandall's APQ-72 had failed completely.

McKeown suddenly realised that they were flying straight down Kep's main runway, and he then noticed two MiG-19s heading towards them. As he turned to engage them it became clear that the MiGs were the bait for a trap when four MiG-17s appeared and one of them rapidly gained a position on McKeown's tail and started firing blazing orange 37 mm shells at him. Two went after Rabb's Phantom II, and he turned tightly, with one MiG-17 following him and shooting. McKeown used his hard-won understanding of the F-4's aerodynamics by employing 'cross-controlling'. He turned increasingly hard in heavy buffeting until the fighter went out of control, performed four rolls and eventually emerged inverted at around 2000 ft – much to Ensch's discomfort.

Quickly recovering his composure, 'Mugs' saw that he now had the MiG-17 right in front of him, and he quickly set up and launched an AIM-9, which the MiG pilot evaded. A second shot at another 'Fresco-C' also went wide, and the 'Rock River' crew then realised that they probably only had one more good AIM-9, as one had failed to tune before take-off. Another MiG-17 turned in behind them, guns blazing, but the aircraft's generally poor gunsight and cannon harmonisation helped to make its heavy shells (a combined weight of fire of 70 lb in a two-second burst) inaccurate. McKeown put negative g on the F-4B and extended his speed brakes, forcing the green-camouflaged MiG to overshoot at close quarters and place itself in line with the final Sidewinder, which McKeown immediately launched. The MiG's tail unit disintegrated and its pilot ejected.

Rabb was having great difficulty in losing a 'Fresco-C' that was following him in a turn, firing all the way until its 40 rounds of ammunition for the single 37mm N-37D and 80 rounds for each of two NR-23 23 mm guns were exhausted. A second MiG then took over and pursued Rabb as he tried to regain some speed. He then made a steep climb, dragging the MiG out in front of McKeown, who had moved into a firing position on it. 'Mugs' selected his fourth (suspect) AIM-9 and surprisingly it acquired the target, launched and turned the 'Fresco-C' into a fireball.

Five days prior to this success, *Midway*'s F-4 crews had claimed their first aerial victories of the cruise. The five MiGs eventually credited to VF-161 in 1972-73 would go some way to offset CVW-5's 15 combat casualties (nine A-7Bs, three F-4Bs, two RF-8Gs and an A-6A) to AAA and SAMs and five operational losses (two F-4Bs, one A-6A, one KA-6D and an A-7B) during almost 11 months on deployment.

The first two successes of the 'Chargers' came from engagements during the afternoon of 18 May. Several hours earlier, VF-213 CO Cdr John Lockhart and wingman Lt Nicholas Criss had been approached at high

Several US pilots claimed to have tangled with the VPAF's small fleet of 925th FR MiG-19S 'Farmer' (Shenyang J-6) 'white bandit' supersonic fighters, although most were actually similar-looking MiG-17s. The only officially confirmed US Navy MiG-19 kills were by two VF-161 crews on 18 May 1972 when the 'Farmers' of Pham Ngoc Tam and Nguyen Thang were shot down during a CVW-15 Alpha strike on an oil storage depot near Haiphong. Both MiG pilots ejected. Fresh from combat (from left to right), Lts Mike 'Taco' Bell and Pat Arwood (flying F-4B BuNo 153915 'Rock River 105') and 'Bart' Bartholomay and Oran Bell (in BuNo 153068 Rock River 110, BuNo 153068) line up for the camera in the squadron ready room on board *Midway*. Brown was standing in for 'Bart's' usual RIO, Lt Rob Anderson, and Arwood, like Bell, was on his first mission into North Vietnam. Both Bell and Bartholomay (who came up with the distinctive VF-161 'black tail' markings) were Topgun graduates, reflected in their bold, coordinated combat tactics in the 18 May fight. 'Bart's' low-altitude kill was made as his fuel levels dropped to critical levels. (*US Navy*)

speed by two 'Fishbed-Js' while on a MiGCAP for a CVW-11 Alpha strike near Kep. After some strenuous turns Criss managed to get behind one MiG and fired an AIM-9 at its maximum range. He then had to break violently as four more MiG-21s were sighted behind them, preventing him from seeing the result of his shot. Black smoke was sighted on the ground, however, and he was credited with a possible kill.

The afternoon mission included a VF-161 MiGCAP 20 miles southeast of Kep, with Lts Henry 'Bart' Bartholomay and Oran Brown in 'Rock River 110' (BuNo 153068) and Lts Patrick Arwood and Mike 'Taco' Bell flying 'Rock River 105' (BuNo 153915, the final F-4B to be ordered). Arwood had only 150 F-4 hours to his name and Bell was on his first trip over North Vietnam. 'Bart' Bartholomay recalled the subsequent MiG engagement as follows;

'We had made one race-track pattern over our CAP station in combat spread. As I looked "through" Pat's plane to check it below, above and his "six o'clock", I saw what appeared to be two "aluminium roof tops" at about 1500 ft AGL [above ground level] seven miles away. As I looked again they moved, so I made the decision to investigate. As we got closer I could see that they were bandits, but it wasn't until we engaged that we identified them as MiG-19s [Shenyang F-6s]. They were heading into the break, having come from China, as we later found out.

'I positioned Pat about 3000 ft above and slightly behind me. My intention was to engage both MiGs as quickly as possible without bringing both our aircraft near ground level. By the time they passed the south end of the airfield I was following behind at 500 ft altitude doing about 600 knots. As I passed over the north end they broke into me and the fight was on. My hope was that the leader would break off so that Pat could fall in behind, which he did. The trail MiG and I were engaged.'

'Taco' Bell saw the MiGs jettison their external tanks and make tight 180-degree turns while Arwood struggled to get a launch tone on an AIM-9 – he eventually resorted to a ballistic Sidewinder to make the MiG pilot turn towards him. 'Bart' Bartholomay tried to follow the other 'white bandit' in a right turn but his speed fell away, so he used the Topgun tactic of moving out of the fight to regain energy before powering back in with a speed advantage.

Arwood made two circuits of the base behind the lead MiG, who then also 'bugged out'. Bartholomay then returned, his speed approaching 500 knots;

'Oran still had our MiG in sight and I picked him up at "ten o'clock", slightly low. He was heading for me, and rather than pulling into him to meet head-on, I kept my speed up and let him progress to a point at which I thought I could get him to overshoot. As he closed I pulled hard into him, up and outside my turn, into an outside barrel roll. As he started to overshoot I popped my speed brakes and pulled back the power. As soon as we were abeam each other, I went to full 'burner and closed the

speed brakes, pulling into him as we both climbed into the vertical. We were no further apart than a couple of hundred feet, bleeding airspeed like it was going out of style. I could see his black helmet and face as he [Pham Ngoc Tam] looked over to check where I was, but we were getting so slow, almost stalling, that I said to Oran, "We've got to get out of here!"

'I knew we weren't going to get a shot, and would be lucky to get out with our lives. But MiGs don't fly well low and slow either, and he had the same idea. As luck would have it I outlasted him by a few seconds and was able to fall into a tight 200 ft trail [behind him] as we both dropped our noses and headed for the deck to gain speed. I was too far inside the Sidewinder envelope for any kind of shot, so I just kept lagging out and pulling back to gain distance. I would have had the opportunity to use guns four times.'

Pat Arwood saw the second MiG-19 (flown by Nguyen Thang Long) apparently seeking to attack 'Rock River 110' from the rear while Bartholomay followed the other one. He pulled in behind the VPAF fighter, released an AIM-9G and saw the MiG's tail disintegrate and the pilot bail out. With his fuel running low, Bartholomay had a final try at his target and fired an AIM-9 without hearing a tone from it. Seconds later, Pham Ngoc Tam jettisoned his canopy and ejected. Bartholomay reflected, 'To this day I don't know whether he was hit by my missile or I just flew him into the ground'.

May 1972 had been a landmark month for the naval Phantom II in its core role as an air-to-air fighter, the results achieved by the units involved validating the new philosophy of ACM introduced by VX-4 and Topgun. The F-4 units' successes would continue, albeit at a reduced rate, for the rest of the year. In May the VPAF had attempted to challenge the US for air superiority over North Vietnam and suffered badly. Soon after 10 May it reverted to earlier *Rolling Thunder* ambush tactics instead, and increased numbers of MiG-21s replaced MiG-17s as first-call interceptors. For the F-4 crews, many of whom usually never saw a MiG, the period of aerial combat was a momentous justification of their role as fighter pilots.

F-4B BuNo 153915, the last F-4B off the production line, was photographed at NAS Miramar just before the commencement of the squadron's second combat deployment on board *Midway* in March 1972 – the unit had only completed its 1971 WestPac a mere five months earlier. On 18 May 1972, with Lts Pat Arwood and Mike Bell at the controls, this aircraft destroyed a MiG-19 with an AIM-9G missile. Lts Bart Bartholomay and Oran Brown downed a second MiG-19 'white bandit' during the same engagement (*Author's collection*)

CHAPTER FIVE

FIGHTING TO THE END

'Rock River 106' (possibly BuNo 153031, which was written off in a deck accident by an errant A-6A on 29 October 1972 – the pilot of the Intruder was killed, as were four deck crew) takes on fuel during a VF-161 strike mission in the autumn of 1972. Placing the retractable refuelling probe into the tanker's 'basket' was usually monitored from the RIO's position while the pilot juggled the throttles to keep the F-4 stable as it became heavier with fuel. Although a RIO's view was restricted by the bulk of the air intakes and his low canopy profile, pilots welcomed the extra space in the F-4 cockpit compared with the more confined 'offices' of other naval jets like the F-8 or A-4, although their vision outside was obviously limited compared with the next generation of fighters. (US Navy)

After the US Navy's 16-to-1 success rate in May 1972, MiG squadrons were less keen to risk combat. Their airfields had been repeatedly bombed and North Vietnam was suffering generally from the *Linebacker I* onslaught. However, they sustained their attempts to fend off US Navy and USAF bombing, and the F-4 squadrons were ready to meet them.

Two VF-51 crews from *Coral Sea* added the third and fourth MiGs to the unit's F-4B-era tally on 11 June using a low-altitude MiGCAP position near a mountain ridge to catch a VPAF MiG-19 flight (misidentified as 'Fresco-Cs' by the Phantom II crews) as it set up its ambush position behind the ridge-line. Cdr Foster Teague, with Lt Ralph Howell, and Lt Winston 'Mad Dog' Copeland, with RIO Lt Don Bouchoux, were vectored into position and informed of the MiGs' approach via instructions from an offshore destroyer – these were relayed to the VF-51 jets by an A-6A Intruder crew. The input from the destroyer was critically important, as both F-4Bs had inoperative radars. Copeland's radio in 'Eagle 113' (BuNo 149457) also failed during the engagement, but on this occasion the 'Mk 1 eyeball' was sufficient.

Howell saw the four MiGs 200 ft above them, and he watched as the jets crossed ahead of them at a range of just three miles. Teague and Copeland turned in behind them and pursued individual targets when the MiG flight broke up. Copeland followed Nguyen Hung Son's lead

MiG into a steep climb, quickly despatching it with an AIM-9G when he attempted to turn in behind Teague's 'Eagle 114' (BuNo 149473). Copeland had to manoeuvre hard to avoid the subsequent explosion. At the same time Teague fired at his target, Nguyen Van Phuc in the No 4 MiG, but the AM-9G went ballistic. Selecting his second missile, he fired again and the MiG disintegrated in flames.

Seconds later he saw a MiG that had escaped to the right re-entering the fight. Turning to a firing position, Teague let loose another AIM-9G that appeared to be homing well for a second

Capt Bill Harris with VF-51's Cdr Foster Teague and Lts Ralph Howell, Winston Copeland and Don Bouchoux on 11 June 1972 after the four Phantom II crewmen downed two MiG-19s (which they had mistakenly claimed were MiG-17s). Unlike the US Navy, the USAF had very little dissimilar air combat training at that time, and its pilots were not used to aggressive air combat manoeuvring. Topgun instructor John Nash described doing ACM in an F-4 as being 'more of an art than a science. The F-4 was a superior ACM airplane, flown by the right guy. The only thing it didn't do well was turn' (*US Navy*)

kill, but the MiG pilot turned more steeply and the missile exploded just behind him, causing noticeable damage. 'Eagle 114' was overshooting fast, so it was not possible to see the outcome and Copeland had already headed out. Teague caught up with him just as a MiG-21 warning was issued and the two F-4Bs crossed the coast. En route, 'Eagle 113' was hit by AAA in the left engine, starting a fire that melted one of the Sparrow missiles, fortunately without detonating it. Copeland managed to make a single-engine landing on board *Coral Sea*, but the battle-worn F-4B was beyond economical repair and never flew again.

Saratoga was seconded from the Atlantic Fleet for a single wartime deployment in April 1972, and this short-notice deployment came as a surprise to VF-31 CO's, MiG killer Cdr 'Geno' Lund (he had claimed a MiG-17 with VF-142 on 30 October 1967);

'The squadron's departure from NAS Oceana was most abrupt. We were all set for a routine Mediterranean cruise when I got a phone call on a Saturday night asking how many planes I could have ready to fly the following Monday. I thought it was one of those periodic drills we had all the time, but I was quickly informed that this was no drill, and that my answer had better be "all 12 of them". Of course it was, and we did just that. One plane was "in check", meaning it was just about completely in parts in the hangar having everything checked out. We even got that one up and ready by Monday.

'Our only combat preparation was carried out in the 30-day transit from Mayport, Florida, to Southeast Asia. My XO, Cdr Jim Flatley III, his prospective XO, Cdr Sam Flynn, and I were the only ones with combat experience, so we had a very intensive training programme to bring everyone up to speed on the situation in Vietnam. We had a Topgun-trained crew already on board, Randy Leddy and his back-seater having taken one of our F-4Js out to Miramar earlier. Cdr Jim Flatley's orders were to assume command in May 1972, so I only got to spend the first line period down south on *Dixie Station* before I had to leave the squadron to him. We had

Red-tailed VF-31 'Tomcatters' F-4J BuNo 157301 in an unusually 'clean' stores configuration. The unit was among those called into action when it became clear that President Richard Nixon, trying to balance the influential voices of the anti-war lobby against his unwillingness to be the first US president to lose a war, would choose a brief, decisive campaign in the form of Operation *Linebacker* in an attempt to end the conflict. (*US Navy*)

a MiG kill marking [from Lund's VF-142 encounter] painted on F-4J AC 101 all the time when I was CO of the squadron, and on AC 102 when I was XO.'

Saratoga duly sustained 13 combat losses, including three F-4Js from VF-103, but downed two MiG-21s in return. Cdr Sam Flynn, on his fourth WestPac cruise, and Lt Bill John got their victory on 21 June whilst flying with 'nugget' pilot Lt Nick 'Star Trek' Strelchuk and Lt Cdr Dave Arnolds as wingmen. At the controls of F-4J 'Bandwagon 106' (BuNo 157307, normally assigned to USAF exchange pilot Capt Ron Williams), they confronted three MiG-21s that were threatening the day's Alpha group, and soon began a climbing and turning duel with one of them while Strelchuk took on a second VPAF fighter. John got a good radar lock-on for an AIM-7 shot, but the missile refused to launch. The MiG pilot continued to manoeuvre skilfully – preventing another missile opportunity, he left the fight. Strelchuk was then warned that he had a MiG-21 behind him, and he had to work hard to avoid three 'Atolls' that were launched at him, losing speed in the process so that the MiG was gradually working its way behind him.

Meanwhile, Flynn, having lost his original opponent, managed to manoeuvre behind the MiG threatening Strelchuk and Arnolds, and he released three AIM-9Ds. The first grazed the MiG without exploding, the second missed but the third entered its tailpipe and destroyed the fighter's engine, forcing the pilot to eject. VF-31 thereby became the second US Navy squadron to have achieved aerial victories in three wars – World War 2, Korea and Vietnam.

MiG opposition declined for the following month, although MiGs remained a serious threat. Indeed, the engagement on 10 July resulted in the loss of VF-103 F-4J 'Clubleaf 212' (BuNo 155803), flown by Lts R I Randall and F J Masterson, after they lost their radar and radio whilst engaged with two MiG-17s flown by Han Vinh Tuong and his

VF-103 'Sluggers' and its carrier *Saratoga* were diverted from a cruise in the Mediterranean to reinforce TF 77 in April 1972. This particular F-4J, BuNo 155803 'Clubleaf 212', became one of the unit's three combat losses, and had the dubious distinction of being the last American aircraft to be destroyed by a MiG-17 and the only one to be shot down exclusively by airborne guns rather than missiles in 1972 (*US Navy*)

wingman Hoang The Thong over Kep. The Phantom II was brought down by 37 mm cannon fire from Tuong's jet, probably combined with an 'Atoll missile' fired by Thong. Both men were captured after ejecting at very low altitude from their blazing F-4, and they were subsequently told that Tuong had failed to return after his MiG hit the ground during the fight. Other VPAF records suggest that it was actually Tuong's wingman who was shot down by a missile fired from an F-4, but the second VF-103 pilot in the section, Lt Al Merriam, did not employ any weapons and made no MiG claim.

VF-103 'Sluggers' struck back on 10 August, but this time on a night-time, single-aircraft MiGCAP. Flying 'Clubleaf 206' (BuNo 157299), Lt Cdr Gene Tucker and Lt(jg) Bruce Edens were launched from Alert Five when a MiG was detected south of Thanh Hoa. After intermittent contact Edens got a solid radar trace at 12 miles and Tucker accelerated behind it in afterburner. Contact was lost again then regained, with the enemy aircraft at 3500 ft. Tucker cleaned off his centreline tank and two triple ejector racks, accelerating to 700 knots and firing two AIM-7E-2s from a distance of two miles. Both missiles caused a massive fireball that was later confirmed as the MiG-21J of Nguyen Ngoc Thien, who did not survive. It was the only confirmed night kill credited to a US Navy F-4, and a victory symbol was marked up on Tucker and Edens' assigned F-4J, BuNo 157305.

Night MiGCAPs for A-6A missions became more necessary in mid-1972 as the VPAF belatedly developed a degree of nightfighter capability with radar-equipped MiG-21PFMs in their attempt to shoot down B-52s. They attracted plenty of SAM opposition, inflicting losses on the Phantom II force. One such aircraft was VF-114 F-4J 'Linfield 211' (BuNo 157262),

VF-74 'Be-devillers' was another Atlantic Fleet F-4J squadron that was temporarily transferred to the Pacific along with its air wing (CVW-8) and carrier (*America*) as part of the *Linebacker* build-up of naval forces, remaining on station until March 1973 and losing only one aircraft (BuNo 153854/AJ 103) in an operational accident that killed the pilot – a night landing on 13 September 1972. This aircraft (BuNo 157280) was also lost in a night landing accident almost five years later, on 15 May 1977, when it rolled over the side of USS *Independence* (CV-62) after taking the rigged barricade whilst the carrier was operating in the Mediterranean. Both the pilot and RIO were killed (*US Navy*)

flown by Cdr John Pitzen and Lt Orland Pender Jr. Performing a MiGCAP for 'Lurking Bertha' A-6 attacks on the northeast rail line on 16 August 1972, the jet was left of the target and crossing the coast when five SA-2s were fired and one downed 'Linfield 211', killing the crew.

Photo-reconnaissance escort missions continued through August 1972, and VF-151 F-4B BuNo 151013 was shot down by an SA-2 near Phu Ly on 27 August while providing MiG protection at 5000 ft. Lt Ted Triebel (on his fourth tour) and Lt(jg) Dave Everett became PoWs as the squadron's only combat losses on its 1972 tour.

Another 'first' occurred on 11 September, when *America*, with CVW-8 embarked, began its third wartime cruise in July 1972 on secondment from Sixth Fleet. Its F-4J squadrons included VF-74 'Be-devillers', at war for the second time after its brief 1967 cruise that was curtailed by the appalling fire on board *Forrestal*. VF-74 was partnered with VMFA-333 'Shamrocks', the first carrier-deployed US Marine Corps F-4 squadron to participate in operations against North Vietnam. Both squadrons began CAP and attack missions in RPs 3 and 4 in July, with night armed reconnaissance sorties being flown from August and flights into RP 6B from September.

The squadron XO, Maj Lee T Lasseter, and his RIO, Capt John D Cummings, were 'Red One', with Capts Scotty Dudley and 'Diamond' Jim Brady, on their first mission into RP 6, as 'Red Two' for a CAP flight controlled by USS *England* (DLG-22) on 11 September. Dudley was still refuelling from a KA-6D tanker when Chief Radarman 'Dutch' Schultz on board *England* reported two MiGs over Phuc Yen airfield. Lasseter and Cummings both had seven-year-long combat records in the F-4, and the latter had been a major contributor to US Marine Corps fighter tactics on BARCAP, TARCAP and escort operations. He had also played a key role in making the AN/AWG-10 more reliable in squadron service.

Although Dudley was short of fuel, they were given a vector to two MiG-21s 61 miles west of them over Phuc Yen, with others near the airfield. Dropping to 3500 ft and leaving another CAP flight to protect the strike group as it attacked a SAM assembly area, they picked up a MiG contact intermittently at 19 miles and low altitude. Cummings steered them into a position about six miles behind a MiG-21 and 'Bear' Lasseter released two AIM-7E-2s as the Phantom II roared over Phuc Yen at 450 knots. The MiG avoided both and remained in their 'ten o'clock' position in a steep turn while Cummings snapped it with his Canon SLR and 100 mm lens (later to be lost in their subsequent ejection).

They were met by numerous SAM warnings and very intense AAA in what was later seen as a MiG and SAM trap that hit one of the F-4Js from the other CAP, which, unknown to them, had been sent to join them. Lasseter stayed behind the MiG, firing his remaining two AIM-7s at very low altitude, where they were subject to ground effect, and releasing two AIM-9Gs (one of which detonated prematurely), but the MiG pilot tightened his turn each time and evaded them all. At that point Dudley's inadequate fuel load reached 'bingo' point and he said he had to leave just as Lasseter finally got a clear AIM-9 shot at the MiG, which, surprisingly, reversed its turn. The AIM-9 blew the fighter apart. Dudley witnessed the nose section of the two-seat MiG-21US continuing to fly abeam of the 'Shamrocks' ' jet. The trainee 921st FR pilot, Maj Dinh Ton, and his Soviet instructor, Vasilij Motlov, ejected safely.

The MiG crew's wingman, who had climbed above the AAA-ridden airfield, returned and fired at Dudley's fuel-starved Phantom II, but 'Red Two' was able to force his opponent to overshoot, and he released an AIM-7E-2 at the 'Fishbed'. At about the same moment Lasseter's 'Shamrock 201' fired its final AIM-9G, which apparently struck the dark-painted MiG-21 without detonating just as Dudley's AIM-7 exploded behind it. Smoke was seen coming from its rear fuselage, but the damaged fighter survived and Lasseter's claim for a second kill was discounted.

VMFA-333 'Shamrocks' F-4J BuNo 154784 was flown by Capts Scott Dudley and 'Diamond Jim' Brady on 11 September 1972 as wingman to Maj 'Bear' Lasseter and Capt John Cummings. In a fight with two MiG-21s, one of the VPAF jets was shot down but both F-4Js were also lost – Lasseter's to a SAM and Dudley's to AAA fired by Phuc Yen's airfield defences (*US Marine Corps*)

With its launching strop under tension and the nose-gear strut extended, VF-111's BuNo 149430 'Old Nick 202' awaits its launch signal aboard *Coral Sea* with a reduced load of bombs and AIM-9 missiles aboard. One of the oldest Phantom IIs assigned to CVW-15 for its eventful 1971-72 WestPac, this aeroplane had completed a previous combat cruise with VF-143 on board *Constellation* in 1968-69 following initial fleet service with VF-14. BuNo 149430 also participated in CVW-15's final Vietnam deployment in 1973, after which it was passed on to VF-121 when VF-111 switched to the F-4N in 1974. The veteran jet was reclassified as a ground trainer at Miramar in October 1975 (*US Navy*)

The exit route for the 'Shamrocks' was directly over the heavy defences around Haiphong, and numerous SAM warnings were transmitted. Dudley saw one missile pass between the two Phantom IIs and warned Lasseter of a second, but his message was blotted out by the frequent radio calls from a TF 77 source and the SA-2 exploded close to their rear fuselage, starting a major fire and lacerating the wings with shrapnel. The doomed F-4 quickly ran out of fuel, at which point Lasseter and Cummings tried to eject. The latter subsequently recalled what happened next;

'The plane pitched forward into a nose-down, inverted spiral with increasing negative g-forces. We were both pressed against our canopies and unable to muster the force necessary to pull either ejection handle. "Bear" [6 ft 3 in tall] reached behind his helmet and began threading his face curtain [from the top of the seat] out an inch at a time. I got my face curtain handle past my helmet and pulled upward and forward along the canopy interior with everything I had. I cracked a cartilage in my rib cage doing it. Neither of us was ever sure who actually triggered the ejection. An armed "Big Mutha" helicopter was there to pick us up and give us a swig of Cold Duck as we rode to spend the night aboard the *England*, the ship that had controlled us. We met "Dutch" Schultz [the MiGCAP controller], dried out the tape in my recorder and pieced together a lot of what had happened. "Bear" and I looked and felt like the dogfight had been a physical encounter with a motorcycle gang. We had numerous cuts and scratches, our backs were stiff from the ejection and the whites of our eyes were cherry red from broken blood vessels caused by the negative g.'

Dudley and Brady also had to abandon their Phantom II (BuNo 154784) when a misdirected tanker failed to meet them in time to prevent a flame-out. The two crews were reunited back aboard *America* the next day.

The incessant BARCAP missions continued to use up much of the F-4 squadrons' time and fuel reserves. The tendency to alleviate the boredom with something more adventurous than music cassettes led to pranks like the one staged by VF-96's Hardy McAllister on a BARCAP. He reported a 'bogie' to 'Red Crown', giving exact headings,

which 'Red Crown' in turn disputed, but still advised the F-4 crew to proceed on their claimed vector of 270 degrees at 20 miles. As McAllister approached the 'contact', he transmitted 'Roger, bearing 270 at 15 miles now, and he's high! He's real high – five miles, four miles, three miles, two miles, one mile. Oh my God, it's so bright! The brilliance! It's unbelievable!' Hardy then turned on his cassette recorder and transmitted a tape of the Hallelujah Chorus.

ENDGAME

The end of *Linebacker I* on 23 October brought renewed hope of a peace deal, but delays occurred as President Nguyen Van Thieu's South Vietnamese government cavilled over the terms of the agreement. Meanwhile, Hanoi hoped that the anti-war protests in the USA would force Nixon to withdraw on unfavourable terms, but also used the opportunity to strengthen its defences once again.

During the pauses in bombing, RA-5Cs and F-4s continued to fly on reconnaissance missions above the 20th parallel, recording the steady military build-up. President Nixon's patience was exhausted by mid-December, and he authorised Operation *Priming Charge* (renamed *Linebacker II*), beginning on 18 December. In stark contrast to the situation under President Johnson, the targeting recommendations by senior USAF and US Navy officers in the war theatre were accepted almost entirely. The majority of the bombing was undertaken by a large force of B-52s (almost half of SAC's fleet) flying 700 sorties from Thailand and Guam, leaving naval forces in a supporting role. Understandably, this proved frustrating to TF 77 personnel, whose strike and fighter aircraft often remained on deck while the USAF filled the skies over Hanoi and Haiphong. Nevertheless, 505 day and night sorties were flown from the five Phantom II-capable

VF-151 F-4Bs bombing above a thick cloud-base under the control of ITT Avionics AN/ALR-92 LORAN-equipped F-4D 66-8776 of the 13th TFS/432nd TRW based at Udorn Royal Thai Air Force Base in late 1972. The AN/ALR-92 system's computer used a chain of ground transmitters to navigate the aircraft to pre-set way-points or target coordinates, potentially giving more accurate results than the F-4D's own inertial navigation system. As an all-weather bombing system, which could be shared by US Navy Phantom IIs that released bombs on a signal from the F-4D, it had limited success (*US Navy*) carriers (*America, Ranger, Saratoga, Enterprise* and *Midway*) and *Oriskany*, with its Crusaders, which made up the enlarged TF 77 force during the 11-day onslaught.

Naval air wings were used to provide limited *Iron Hand* defence suppression with A-6B Intruders, A-4F Skyhawks and A-7E Corsair IIs, together with unescorted nocturnal A-6 strikes in the Haiphong area, hitting petroleum/oil/lubricants depots, barracks, railway yards and dock facilities between B-52 attacks. Ten SAM sites in the Haiphong area were attacked on the night of 20 December by aircraft from *Ranger* and *America*, but the sheer number of SA-2s fired from other sites still meant that six B-52s were lost. The SAM site attacks drew considerable opposition, helping to run down the enemy's extensive stocks of the missiles. Naval aircraft also re-seeded the minefields laid in Operation *Pocket Money*.

As most of the attacks were flown by night, there was little opportunity for visual bombing by F-4s, and 90 per cent of the 20,000 tons of bombs dropped during *Linebacker II* were radar-aimed, with only 2.6 per cent being dropped visually. Later analysis showed that visually sighted bombs were usually far more accurate than radar-aimed ordnance, particularly when dropped under the guidance of LORAN (long-range navigation), as much of the F-4s' ordnance was during the war. Far better results were obtainable by the Paveway LGBs that were available in very limited quantities, but only for USAF Phantom IIs. They achieved a 20 ft CEP, but were used for only 0.2 per cent of the attacks.

The weather was also an important factor in limiting operations by aircraft that were not considered 'all-weather'. The target area was covered by a heavy overcast extending up to 6000 ft for most of the 11 days of *Linebacker II*, leaving only a 12-hour slot in which low-altitude aircraft other than the radar-equipped A-6A and F-111A could bomb visually. RA-5Cs also flew pre-strike, BDA and passive ECM missions with F-4 escort, although Phantom IIs were often hard pressed to keep up with the clean, fast-moving Vigilantes due to their external stores. They carried only half of the RA-5C's internal fuel but had almost the same engines, so 'draggy' external tanks were essential to match the cleanly configured 'Viggie's' range.

The RVAH squadrons' passive ECM orbits offshore during B-52 raids also allowed them to record radar and radio intelligence passing between North Vietnamese sources. SAM sites' 'Fan Songs' were jammed by US Marine Corps EA-6A Intruders and US Navy EA-6B Prowler ECM aircraft, the latter having begun operations with *America*'s VAQ-132 in June 1972.

Pre-strike and BDA missions were invariably hazardous for RA-5C crews, with 26 being lost and 25 crew killed. Their escorting F-4s were also at risk, even though they could make constant 'jinking' manoeuvres to avoid ground fire while the reconnaissance aircraft had to fly straight and level. RA-5C crews usually flew with at least minimum afterburner to preserve speed and reduce their smoke trail, making it harder for F-4s to keep up.

VMFA-333 F-4J 'Shamrock 210' (BuNo 153885), flying from *America*, took a direct hit by 85 mm flak on 23 December while escorting RVAH-6

Vigilante 'Fieldgoal 603' during a mission to find a North Vietnamese torpedo-boat base. The Phantom II immediately caught fire and went into a steep dive from about 3000 ft. Its crew, Lt Col John Cochran (the squadron CO) and RIO Maj H S Carr, bailed out just offshore from Hon Gay, and they were rescued under fire by a 'Big Mother' HH-3A helicopter, although Cochran's back was injured during ejection. 'Fieldgoal 603' made low-level passes across the beach to draw enemy fire and a VA-86 A-7 dropped Rockeye to take out a heavy gun that was threatening the rescue attempt. It was the only loss of a carrier-based F-4 during *Linebacker II*.

Despite the best efforts of US Navy *Iron Hand* strike aircraft and USAF *Wild Weasel* F-105Gs during the nightly B-52 assaults, more than 1250 SA-2 missiles were fired at US aircraft, destroying 15 B-52s and damaging 25 others. In retrospect, some analysts estimated that a more concentrated effort to destroy the defences, particularly the 30 well-stocked SAM sites, in advance of the operation might have reduced the casualties, but resources for this purpose were limited and any element of surprise would have been lost. In fact, the citizens of Hanoi and Haiphong had been told by their leaders to expect such an onslaught since the beginning of the war eight years previously. Of the 13 SAM sites that were bombed by B-52s and tactical aircraft dropping 1300 bombs, the average destruction was only ten per cent. On 26 December alone some 100 sorties by F-4s, A-6s, A-7s and F-111s were directed at SAM and radar sites. Similarly, the five MiG airfields that were priority targets for 141 tactical strike sorties only suffered a nine per cent destruction rate despite repeated attacks. Much greater damage had been inflicted on them by US Navy and USAF attacks during *Linebacker I*. One consequence of the airfield attacks was a drastic reduction in MiG encounters, with only two MiG kills by US Navy Phantom IIs in December 1972 and January 1973 – the same number claimed by B-52 tail-gunners.

F-4J BuNo 158373 was the CAG aircraft for VF-154 'Black Knights' for four years in the mid-1970s (including during two consecutive WestPacs to Vietnam). The squadron completed four F-4J combat tours with CVW-2 on board *Ranger* from 1968 to 1973, with a fifth being undertaken in 1974. The unit was partnered with VF-21 throughout this time, and it lost only one aircraft, in an operational accident, when F-4J BuNo 155750 failed to complete a successful catapult launch for a BARCAP mission and crashed into the sea on 11 January 1970, killing pilot Lt Terence Ryan. Demonstrating the fortuitous nature of MiG encounters, VF-154 claimed no aerial victories on any of its six CVW-2 deployments, including two with F-4Bs (*Author's collection*)

As *Linebacker II* continued to pound the VPAF's bases, MiG activity inevitably declined. MiGCAP missions were typically flown offshore, although during *Linebacker II* some were set up over land to provide further protection for the B-52s. F-4 crews on these missions were amazed at the numbers of SA-2s being fired at the cells of B-52s as they flew straight and level, in trail formation, on very predictable routes.

There were two more aerial victories for US Navy F-4 flyers, with VF-142 claiming the penultimate MiG of the war on 28 December – the day that the 90th, and last, American aircraft (officially confirmed by US records) to be shot down by a MiG crashed into the sea. RVAH-13 RA-5C 'Flint 603' (BuNo 156633) from *Enterprise*, flown by Lt Cdr Al Agnew and Lt Michael Haifley, was claimed by 927th FR pilot Hoang Tan Hung, the Vigilante crew being killed. Their VF-143 F-4J escort had given a MiG warning, but Agnew was not able to turn his jet hard enough to avoid the pair of 'Atolls' that another Phantom II crew had seen heading for his aircraft. It was the only RA-5C to be lost to a MiG.

Lt(jg)s Scott Davis and Jeff Ulrich were both inexperienced in combat, and they were flying as wingman to Cdr Don Riggs, the CO for the 'Ghostriders', on 28 December. 'Red Crown' on board *Chicago* had reported MiG-21s launching to meet the strike force. There was some confusion about the fighters' location, but Davis got a contact and visual ID at eight miles, although his radar would not lock on to the target. He approached closer for an AIM-9 shot, but the MiG was speeding ahead at 550 knots out of range, and it had shot down the RA-5C before Davis could attempt to fire. The MiG evaded the missile and turned back towards Davis' 'Dakota 214' (BuNo 155846).

Two other VF-142 F-4Js duly took up the chase and fired at the silver MiG-21 as it escaped into clouds. Davis calculated where it would reappear, and it emerged at very low altitude, travelling at 600 knots in the direction of home. The two fighters continued a series of shallow turns as Davis maintained the pursuit and

VF-151 'Vigilantes' F-4B BuNo 152258 was photographed at Miramar shortly after the squadron had returned from its final combat cruise with CVW-5 in April 1973, and just before the unit's conversion to the F-4N. The eye-catching decor extended to the aircraft's wingtips, replacing the more basic red rudder stripes worn for VF-151's earlier cruises on board *Constellation* and *Coral Sea*. From October 1973 the squadron and CVW-5 were forward deployed to Atsugi, Japan. BuNo 152258 had previously seen action in Vietnam from 1966 whilst serving with VMFA-323 and then VMFA-542. Upgraded to F-4N specification, the jet served with VF-21 until withdrawn from the frontline in 1982 and converted into a QF-4N. It was expended shortly thereafter (*Author's collection*)

eventually fired again. His Sidewinder exploded a few feet behind the fleeing MiG without apparent damage, but Davis observed that the enemy jet eventually became quite unstable at the 50-100 ft altitude at which they were flying and impacted the ground, killing Hoang Tam Hung. This loss confirmed the US Navy's 12-to-1 kill/loss ratio for 1972, with 24 MiGs downed and two F-4s lost to them.

The final aerial engagement came on 12 January 1973 when VF-161 F-4B BuNo 153045, flown by Lt Vic Kovaleski and Lt(jg) Jim Wise caught a grey-and-green camouflaged 923rd FR MiG-17 while on a BARCAP. The crew took advantage of more permissive RoE, allowing them to pursue the MiG beyond the 20th parallel, although (according to "Bart" Bartholomay) it took 'three or four passes for the controller to get them hooked up on the MiG'. A single AIM-9 shot took off the fighter's tail and pilot Luu Kim Ngo ejected, but his parachute apparently did not deploy. Kovaleski was shot down by 85 mm AAA two days later while on a *Blue Tree* escort mission in Bartholomay's MiG killer BuNo 153068. He and RIO Ens D H Plautz were recovered.

Operations continued through January as a peace deal was argued out, and so did F-4 losses. On 27 January, the day that the treaty was actually signed, Cdr Harley H Hall and Lt Cdr Philip Kientzler's VF-143 F-4J BuNo 155768 was hit by flak while attacking trucks near Quang Tri. Control failure and fire forced them to eject, and Kientzler, with 500 combat missions behind him, was captured, becoming the last US Navy PoW in Vietnam. Cdr Hall, former leader of the *Blue Angels* and a legend in the F-4 community, was allegedly killed by a North Vietnamese soldier, like the crew of their OV-10A FAC aircraft that day, although his true fate remains in doubt. The last loss of all resulted from a tragic mid-air collision between two VF-21 F-4Js during a 30 January BARCAP. One crew, Lt James Duensing and Lt(jg) Roy Haviland, died and the other two men (Lt(jg) Reid and Lt Beaver) escaped from their crashing Phantom II, these jets being *Ranger's* final wartime losses.

By 15 January the hurriedly reconvened peace negotiations yielded acceptable results and US combat operations in Vietnam were ended. A ceasefire agreement was signed on 27 January, enabling the return of 600 PoWs to commence on 12 February. Operation *End Sweep* during that month removed the mines from Haiphong's waters, although the task was frequently halted by North Vietnamese ceasefire violations in South Vietnam and Cambodia. At times it seemed to some US Navy personnel in the area that further air attacks were a possibility.

Constellation, still with VF-92 and VF-96 embarked as part of CVW-9, returned to *Yankee Station* on 1 February and began four days of combat over Laos, where the Peace Accord did not become effective until 21 February. VF-96 CO Cdr Dwight Timm flew the squadron's last combat mission on 11 February, after which the air wing flew BARCAP missions for Operation *End Sweep*. The possibility of further action required the F-4s to be fitted with progressive 'Charger Blue' updated ECM equipment to protect them from SA-3 'Goa' missiles before the carrier's seventh and final line period in August 1973. Most US Navy F-4s had received the ITEK AN/ALR-45 countermeasures receiving set and

Raytheon AN/ALR/50 radar receiving set in 1970, and additional ECM modifications begun in 1972-73 added the Sanders AN/ALQ-126 noise deception jamming system.

Within three years the North Vietnamese had ignored the peace deal and moved south in force. In April 1975 Operation *Frequent Wind*, the final evacuation of US personnel from Saigon, took place as North Vietnamese tanks entered the city and *Midway*, loaded with nine USAF rescue helicopters, and *Enterprise* were ordered back to the South China Sea, with *Coral Sea* and *Hancock* (with US Marine Corps CH-53A helicopters embarked) also on call. US Navy fighter squadrons, including the first examples of the F-4's successor, the F-14A Tomcats of VF-1 and VF-2 assigned to CVW-14 and embarked in *Enterprise*, provided cover for the helicopters as they airlifted US evacuees and dependents. *Midway* alone accepted 2074 refugees in the first 24 hours of the operation. On some flights up to 80 refugees were crammed into helicopters

VF-111 adopted a more modest sunburst scheme, as seen here on BuNo 150648, for its 1973 war cruise. The squadron, still embarked in *Coral Sea*, returned to the area in 1975 for Operation *Frequent Wind* (the evacuation of Saigon). Tactics devised by VX-4 from 1966 and later incorporated in the Topgun syllabus favoured manoeuvring in the vertical plane, where the F-4 had a thrust-to-weight advantage over the MiG-17, rather than engaging in horizontal turning fights where the MiG could easily out-turn the Phantom II. A MiG-21MF was capable of out-running an F-4J at low altitude. BuNo 150648 was also a combat veteran from the 1960s, having served with US Marine Corps units based in South Vietnam. It too was upgraded into an F-4N post-war, and sent to MASDC in late 1977 (*US Navy*)

designed for 12 soldiers. Another 80,000 were rescued by other US Navy ships, ending the role of the Seventh Fleet in trying to save those South Vietnamese who resisted the communist take-over.

Seventeen US Navy carriers had participated in the Vietnam War between 1968 and 1973, making 72 cruises and providing up to 400 aircraft at once. The sacrifices were considerable – 317 aircrew were killed and 854 aircraft were lost to all causes. Despite the relatively small bomb-loads compared with B-52s or F-111As (which could carry four times the bomb-load of a carrier-borne F-4) necessitated by carrier operations, naval aircraft delivered 1.5 million tons of ordnance, which was about a quarter of the total wartime amount. Multi-role F-4 units were a vital component in that process, either by delivering bombs themselves or protecting other attack, reconnaissance and radar control aircraft.

APPENDICES

US Navy Phantom II Unit Deployments to TF 77 1969-73

Unit	Model	Code/Modex	Carrier Air Wing	Carrier	Deployment dates
VF-21 'Freelancers'					
VF-21	F-4J	NE 1	CVW-2	USS *Ranger* (CVA-61)	14/10/69 to 1/6/70
VF-21	F-4J	NE 1	CVW-2	USS *Ranger* (CVA-61)	27/10/70 to 17/6/71
VF-21	F-4J	NE 2	CVW-2	USS *Ranger* (CVA-61)	6/11/72 to 22/6/73
VF-31 'Tomcatters'					
VF-31	F-4J	AC 1	CVW-3	USS *Saratoga* (CVA/CV-60)	11/4/72 to 13/2/73
VF-51 'Screaming Eagles'					
VF-51	F-4B	NL 1	CVW-15	USS *Coral Sea* (CVA-43)	12/11/71 to 17 7/72
VF-51	F-4B	NL 1	CVW-15	USS *Coral Sea* (CVA-43)	9/3/73 to 8/11/73
VF-74 'Be-Devillers'					
VF-74	F-4J	AJ 1	CVW-8	USS *America* (CV-66)	5/6/72 to 24/3/73
VF-92 'Silver Kings'					
VF-92	F-4J	NG 2	CVW-9	USS *Enterprise* (CVAN-65)	6/1/69 to 2/7/69
VF-92	F-4J	NG 2	CVW-9	USS *America* (CVA-66)	10/4/70 to 21/12/70
VF-92	F-4J	NG 2	CVW-9	USS *Constellation* (CVA-64)	1/10/71 to 1/7/72
VF-92	F-4J	NG 2	CVW-9	USS *Constellation* (CVA-64)	5/1/73 to 11/10/73
VF-96 'Fighting Falcons'					
VF-96	F-4J	NG 1	CVW-9	USS *Enterprise* (CVAN-65)	6/1/69 to 2/7/69
VF-96	F-4J	NG 1	CVW-9	USS *America* (CVA-66)	10/4/70 to 21/12/70
VF-96	F-4J	NG 1	CVW-9	USS *Constellation* (CVA-64)	1/10/71 to 1/7/72
VF-96	F-4J	NG 1	CVW-9	USS *Constellation* (CVA-64)	5/1/73 to 11/10/73
VF-103 'Sluggers'					
VF-103	F-4J	AC 2	CVW-3	USS *Saratoga* (CVA/CV-60)	11/4/72 to 13/2/73
VF-111 'Sundowners'					
VF-111	F-4B	NL 2	CVW-15	USS *Coral Sea* (CVA-43)	12/11/71 to 17/7/72
VF-111	F-4B	NL 2	CVW-15	USS *Coral Sea* (CVA-43)	9/3/73 to 8/11/73
VF-114 'Aardvarks'					
VF-114	F-4B	NH 2	CVW-11	USS *Kitty Hawk* (CVA-63)	30/12/68 to 4/9/69
VF-114	F-4J	NH 2	CVW-11	USS *Kitty Hawk* (CVA-63)	6/11/70 to 17/7/71
VF-114	F-4J	NH 2	CVW-11	USS *Kitty Hawk* (CVA-63)	17/2/72 to 28/11/72
VF-142 'Ghostriders'					
VF-142	F-4B	NK 2	CVW-14	USS *Constellation* (CVA-64)	29/5/68 to 31/1/69
VF-142	F-4J	NK 2	CVW-14	USS *Constellation* (CVA-64)	11/8/69 to 8/5/70
VF-142	F-4J	NK 2	CVW-14	USS *Enterprise* (CVAN-65)	11/6/71 to 12/2/72
VF-142	F-4J	NK 2	CVW-14	USS *Enterprise* (CVAN-65)	12/9/72 to 12/6/73

VF-143 'Pukin' Dogs'

VF-143	F-4B	NK 3	CVW-14	USS *Constellation* (CVA-64)	29/5/68 to 31/1/69
VF-143	F-4J	NK 3	CVW-14	USS *Constellation* (CVA-64)	11/8/69 to 8/5/70
VF-143	F-4J	NK 1	CVW-14	USS *Enterprise* (CVAN-65)	11/6/71 to 12/2/72
VF-143	F-4J	NK 1	CVW-14	USS *Enterprise* (CVAN-65)	12/9/72 to 12/6/73

VF-151 'Vigilantes'

VF-151	F-4B	NL 1	CVW-15	USS *Coral Sea* (CVA-43)	7/9/68 to 12/4/69
VF-151	F-4B	NL 1	CVW-15	USS *Coral Sea* (CVA-43)	23/9/69 to 1/7/70
VF-151	F-4B	NF 2	CVW-5	USS *Midway* (CVA-41)	16/4/71 to 6/11/71
VF-151	F-4B	NF 2	CVW-5	USS *Midway* (CVA-41)	10/4/72 to 3/3/73

VF-154 'Black Knights'

VF-154	F-4J	NE 2	CVW-2	USS *Ranger* (CVA-61)	26/10/68 to 17/5/69
VF-154	F-4J	NE 2	CVW-2	USS *Ranger* (CVA-61)	14/10/69 to 1/6/70
VF-154	F-4J	NE 2	CVW-2	USS *Ranger* (CVA-61)	27/10/70 to 17/6/71
VF-154	F-4J	NE 1	CVW-2	USS *Ranger* (CVA-61)	16/11/72 to 22/6/73

VF-161 'Chargers'

VF-161	F-4B	NL 2	CVW-15	USS *Coral Sea* (CVA-43)	7/9/68 to 12/4/69
VF-161	F-4B	NL 2	CVW-15	USS *Coral Sea* (CVA-43)	23/9/69 to 1/7/70
VF-161	F-4B	NF 1	CVW-5	USS *Midway* (CVA-41)	16/4/71 to 6/11/71
VF-161	F-4B	NF 1	CVW-5	USS *Midway* (CVA-41)	10/4/72 to 3/3/73

VF-213 'Black Lions'

VF-213	F-4B	NH 1	CVW-11	USS *Kitty Hawk* (CVA-63)	30/12/68 to 4/9/69
VF-213	F-4J	NH 1	CVW-11	USS *Kitty Hawk* (CVA-63)	6/11/70 to 17/7/71
VF-213	F-4J	NH 1	CVW-11	USS *Kitty Hawk* (CVA-63)	17/2/72 to 28/11/72

VMFA-333 'Shamrocks'

VMFA-333	F-4J	AJ 2	CVW-8	USS *America* (CV-66)	5/6/72 to 24/3/73

COLOUR PLATES

1
F-4J-39-MC BuNo 155891/NE 107 of VF-21, USS *Ranger* (CVA-61), June 1970

This fighter was assigned to Lt(jg)s D E Peterson and E A Mack. With a paint finish that bears the evidence of a long combat cruise (the fifth, for VF-21), this hardworking F-4J demonstrates the markings scheme that was modified from the decor used on the F-4Bs of the 'Freelancers' up to the summer of 1968. VF-21 transitioned to the F-14A in 1984 after 22 years with Phantom IIs, and this example was withdrawn from service three years later after conversion to F-4S standard in January 1983 and a period with VMFA-312.

2
F-4J-47-MC BuNo 158378/NE 200 of VF-21, USS *Ranger* (CVA-61), June 1973

This aircraft, assigned at the time to CVW-2 CO Cdr Roger Massey, also carried the name Rear Admiral Wes McDonald on its aft canopy rails. The latter was *Ranger*'s Carrier Battle Group Commander, his two-star pennant adorning the jet's splitter plate. As CO of VA-56 on board *Ticonderoga*, McDonald had led the first air strike – Operation

Pierce Arrow – against North Vietnam on 5 August 1964 following the Gulf of Tonkin incident. CAG F-4J of the 'Freelancers' for the best part of ten years, BuNo 158378 replaced BuNo 155900 in this role after VF-21's participation in CVW-2's 1970-71 combat cruise on board CVA-61. For much of the 1972-73 WestPac deployment, the fighter was assigned to CAG Cdr C J Cellar, who handed over command of CVW-2 to Cdr Roger Massey on 11 June 1973 – just 11 days before the cruise ended. The squadron converted to the F-4N in 1981, and this aircraft, the penultimate F-4J off the production line, was passed to US Marine Corps training squadron VMFAT-101 in 1982 and then VMFA-212, prior to being withdrawn from service in 1985.

3
F-4J-43-MC BuNo 157293/AC 100 of VF-31 'Tomcatters', USS *Saratoga* (CV-60), August 1972

Depicted here bearing a full CAP consignment of AIM-7E and AIM-9G missiles, this F-4J served as VF-31's CAG jet during the *Linebacker* period at a time when Cdr Richard P 'Deke' Bordone was CAG of CVW-3 for its sole wartime cruise. The following year this Phantom II was assigned to Cdr Sam Flynn and Lt Bill John as AC 101, although it was not the aircraft in which they achieved their June 1972 MiG kill. VF-102 took it over in 1975 as AG 101, assigned to Cdr L 'Ferg' Norton and Lt Sam A Montgomery. By 1977 BuNo 157293 had been transferred to VF-11 as AA 112, and in 1980 it was in low-visibility camouflage with VF-102 as AE 110. The jet was converted to F-4S configuration in October 1981 and eventually acquired by the Texas Air Museum in Slaton, Texas, after service with VMFA-122 as DC 11 and withdrawal from frontline use in September 1985.

4
F-4J-36-MC BuNo 155864/AC 112 of VF-31, USS *Saratoga* (CV-60), December 1972

This aircraft was assigned to Lt Nick 'Star Trek' Strelchuck (the squadron's communications officer in 1972) and Lt(jg) 'Bull' Walker during *Saratoga*'s ten-month combat cruise in 1972-73. Strelchuck (with Lt Cdr Dave Arnolds as his RIO) was part of a two-aircraft CAP with Cdr Flynn and Lt John on 21 June 1972 that developed into a strenuous missile duel with three MiG-21s and resulted in one of the 'Fishbeds' being downed by Flynn and John. This aircraft is armed with Mk 20 Rockeye II anti-armour ordnance, introduced in 1968, in Mk 7 dispensers. The shaped-charge, dart-like bomblets were particularly effective for *Iron Hand* flak suppression missions. This F-4J, 'Bandwagon 112', which also flew with VF-84, VF-154 and VMFA-321 prior to being upgraded to F-4S standard in June 1980, and then with VMFA-134, was withdrawn from use in November 1991 and subsequently converted into a QF-4S drone. It was duly destroyed by an air-to-air missile whilst serving as a target aircraft on 21 December 2000.

5
F-4B-26-MC BuNo 153027/NL 103 of VF-51, USS *Coral Sea* (CVA-43), June 1972

Formerly with VF-114 (one of whose MiG kills is recorded on the splitter plate, although BuNo 153037 was actually responsible for that victory on 24 April 1967), this F-4B also flew with VF-32, VF-301, VF-103 (CAG aircraft) and VF-154 (as an F-4N) until 1982, when it was placed in storage at Davis-Monthan AFB's Military Aircraft Storage and Disposition Center (MASDC) in Tucson, Arizona. The Phantom II was crewed by Lt Cdr Jerry B 'Devil' Houston and Lt(jg) Dave Dixon during its VF-51 career. Houston's own MiG kill, with Lt Kevin Moore as RIO, was achieved in BuNo 150456. The striking 'supersonic can-opener' decor was chosen as a conscious antithesis of low-visibility camouflage and as a challenge to potential adversaries. The aircraft has the AN/APR-25/APR-30 RHAW antenna additions.

6
F-4B-12-MC BuNo 150417/NL 107 of VF-51, USS *Coral Sea* (CVA-43), August 1971

Assigned to Lt Winston Copeland and Lt(jg) Dale Arends, this F-4B sustained control failure during a BARCAP mission off North Vietnam on 3 March 1972 and Lts Moore and Westfall had to abandon it. Copeland and Arends were then given BuNo 151398 (adorned with *MAD DOG* titling, inspired by Copeland's nickname, on its fin cap), which Lts Ken Cannon and Roy Morris used to destroy a MiG-17 on 10 May 1972. Copeland and Lt Don Bouchoux used BuNo 149457 for their MiG victory on 11 June. NL 107 had previously served with VF-101 and VF-142 (twice), as well as having completed two years of combat with VF-96 (1966-67).

7
F-4J-29-MC BuNo 153787/AJ 112 of VF-74, USS *America* (CV-66), April 1973

VF-74's first wartime cruise in 1967 was curtailed by a disastrous fire on board *Forrestal* just five days after CVA-59 had made its combat debut, and the 'Be-devillers' did not return to TF 77 until June 1972. By then the unit had switched from F-4Bs to the J-model Phantom II, and it had also changed air wings, having joined CVW-8 from CVW-17. Aircrew names were usually removed from canopy frames at the end of the cruise, pending the aircraft's re-assignment – this jet remained with VF-74, which was in turn transferred back to CVW-17 for a six-month Mediterranean cruise on board *Forrestal* from March 1974. BuNo 153787 was transferred to the US Marine Corps in 1981, serving with VMFA-333 and VMFA-451 until it was upgraded into an F-4S and supplied to US Navy Reserve unit VF-202 in 1984. Eventually converted into a QF-4S drone, the jet was expended on 21 July 2000.

8
F-4J-34-MC BuNo 155772/NG 213 of VF-92, USS *Enterprise* (CVAN-65), July 1969

Assigned to Lt(jg)s Scott Finkboner and Gene Williamson, this F-4J participated in the squadron's fifth WestPac cruise – the first of three with the F-4J after conversion from the F-4B variant. It had a long period of service with VF-92, preceded and followed by time with VMFA-333 and VFMA-235, respectively. The 'Silver Kings' operated from five different aircraft carriers during the war, losing only two F-4Js in combat. Partnered with VF-96, VF-92 was a major participant in the Vietnam conflict from 1964 to the end of 1973. Nevertheless, both units were disestablished in 1975.

9
F-4J-34-MC BuNo 155780/NG 205 of VF-92, USS *Constellation* (CVA-64), 1971-72

VF-92 retained its 'Silver King' tail markings for the 1972 cruise, moving to an all-yellow tail with a black ace motif in 1973 for yet another WestPac deployment on board *Constellation* with CVW-9. The 'Connie' ended the war as the carrier with the most MiG kills, totalling 15 aerial victories, eight of them by the US Navy's top-scoring squadron, VF-96. Multiple racks loaded with Mk 82 bombs, as depicted here, were often used for TPQ radar bombing sorties, but some air-to-air weapons were usually uploaded too. This aircraft became one of the squadron's two F-4J operational losses when it had to ditch during a mission from *Constellation* on 28 October 1972.

10
F-4J-34-MC BuNo 155769/NG 106 of VF-96, USS *Constellation* (CVA-64), 1972-74

Assigned to Lts Charles de Gruy and Paul Donalson, this F-4J is laden with Mk 82 bombs and a mixed load of Sidewinder and Sparrow missiles. It also carries a ubiquitous centreline fuel tank. Lt Donalson was RIO in this aircraft in 1972, teamed with Lt Cdr Al Liner. With Lts Matt Connelly and Tom Blonski aboard, 'Showtime 106' shot down two MiG-17s on 10 May 1972. The jet remained in the squadron until 1974, when it moved to VF-121 for training duties and then to US Navy Reserve squadron VF-302 'Stallions' as an F-4S. It was finally struck off after a crash-landing at El Paso airport, in Texas, in April 1983.

11
F-4J-35-MC BuNo 155792/NG 107 of VF-96, USS *Constellation* (CVA-64), 1971-72

Armed with Mk 20 Rockeye II, AIM-9G and AIM-7E-2 weaponry, 'Showtime 107' was assigned to Lts Randy Cunningham and Les Smith. The jet has the squadron's eight MiG kill markings on its intake ramp and the Adm Joseph C Clifton Trophy (1971-72) emblem on the upper fuselage just aft of the cockpit. BuNo 155792 was a lucky aircraft in that the F-4Js with serial numbers immediately before and after it were lost in the deck fire on board *Enterprise* in January 1969. After VF-96's disestablishment, the jet flew with VMFA-333, continuing in service as an F-4S until November 1985.

12
F-4J-44-MC BuNo 157305/AC 203 of VF-103, USS *Saratoga* (CV-60), autumn 1972

This Phantom II was assigned to Lt Cdr Gene Tucker and Lt(jg) Bruce Edens, although it was not the one they flew for their mission on 10 August 1972 when they claimed the only night MiG kill of the war. The squadron received some late-production F-4Js for its solitary WestPac cruise in 1972-73, joining an expanded TF 77 to counter renewed North Vietnamese incursions into the south of the country. The 'golden arrow' tail motif was inherited from the squadron's F-4B days, and it continued to be applied to VF-103 jets in various forms for the rest of its Phantom II-operating years until 1983, when the unit re-equipped with the F-14A. This F-4J ('Club Leaf 203' in 1972) was subsequently transferred to the 'Sluggers'' regular partner squadron, VF-102, with whom it served from 1975 to 1980 (including a brief period with VF-101). Upgraded into an F-4S in the early 1980s, the aircraft was then used to train replacement aircrew with VF-171 'Aces' before ending its days with the US Marine Corps – BuNo 157305 was struck off charge at MCAS Kaneohe Bay, Hawaii, on 2 March 1988.

13
F-4J-35-MC BuNo 155824/AC 213 of VF-103, USS *Saratoga* (CV-60), late 1972

Lt(jg)s Bob Randall and Paul Bower were assigned to this F-4J, the latter serving with the 'Sluggers' from 1970 to 1973 – he was the unit's admin/personnel officer in 1972-73. Bob Randall and Lt Fred Masterson were shot down by cannon fire from a MiG-17 during a dogfight over Kep airfield on 10 July 1972, their jet (VF-103 F-4J BuNo 155803) being the last loss of a US aircraft to a 'Fresco-C', and the only one in 1972 attributed to MiG-17 gunfire. The MiG pilot, Hanh Vinh Tuong, was apparently shot down and killed by a missile from another F-4J during the same mission, although no kill was claimed by a US crew that day. Randall and Masterson remained in captivity until March 1973. Passed on to VF-102 in 1975, BuNo 155824 was transferred to VF-74 the following year and written off on 17 August 1978 in a crash on board *Forrestal* whilst still with the unit.

14
F-4B-13-MC BuNo 150466/NL 204 of VF-111, NAS Miramar, June 1971

Depicted during the squadron's work-up on the F-4B before its first deployment with the aircraft on board *Coral Sea* in November 1971, this F-4B lacks crew details and a carrier name – both would be applied prior to CVW-15's embarkation in CVA-43 later in the year. The 'Sundowners' had been a fiercely proud F-8 squadron until early 1971, making seven WestPac cruises with the Crusader from five different carriers. Having transitioned to the F-4B, the unit remained with CVW-15 until its disestablishment in 1995 after 36 years of service. This F-4B also had a long, active career between its first flight in November 1962 and service withdrawal in May 1984.

15
F-4B-15-MC BuNo 151464/NL 211 of VF-111, USS *Coral Sea* (CVA-43), November 1973

Seen at NAS Miramar at the conclusion of its second F-4 cruise, this 'Sundowners' Phantom II has lost its crew nameplates from its canopies. It also shows off the revised tail markings that were adopted prior to restoration of the full 'sunburst' on the unit's F-4Ns from 1974 to 1978 and carried over to the squadron's F-14A era. During the Vietnam War VF-111 flew 12,500 combat sorties. Its second *Coral Sea* WestPac, from March to November 1973, was officially a 'Vietnam cruise' as hostilities after the January 1973 ceasefire continued until North Vietnam took Saigon in April 1975. BuNo 151464 spent much of its service career with the US Marine Corps, seeing combat in Vietnam with VMFA-323 and VMFA-115 prior to joining VF-111. Upgraded to F-4N specification post-war, the jet was with VMFA-323 when it was written off in a non-flying accident on board *Coral Sea* on 19 February 1980.

16
F-4J-41-MC BuNo 157261/NH 210 of VF-114, USS *Kitty Hawk* (CVA-63), October 1971

Using very similar markings to those worn by its F-4Bs, VF-114 converted to F-4Js in 1970, retaining the Phantom until it transitioned to the F-14A in 1975. The squadron's second combat cruise with the J-model began on 17 February 1972 and lasted until 17 November that same year, during which time it lost two jets in combat and had four aircrew killed. In 1961 VF-114 was the first deployable Pacific Fleet squadron to receive Phantom IIs, and the first of six combat cruises, all on board *Kitty Hawk* with CVW-11, began in October 1965. Four MiGs were claimed during that time. This F-4J spent the majority of its post-'Aardvark' career with US Marine Corps units, including VMFAT-101, VMFA-321 and VMFA-212. Withdrawn from use in November 1991, the aircraft was converted into a QF-4S drone and eventually expended.

17
F-4B-26-MC BuNo 153026/NH 203 VF-114, USS *Kitty Hawk* (CVA-63), December 1970

Assigned to Lt Cdr John Farnsworth, this Phantom II, nicknamed *PATTY* (its name was applied in black to the red/black shield on the splitter plate) is seen towards the end of the squadron's F-4B period. It has the AN/APR-30 ECM fittings, although *Kitty Hawk*'s Phantom IIs had the later APR-25 Shoehorn equipment by this time, using the same fittings. The distinctive 'Zot' aardvark logo on the fin originated when the squadron XO, Cdr Roscoe Trout, requested it from *B.C.* comic strip creator Johnny Hart. BuNo 153026 was subsequently passed on to VF-151 in 1971 and upgraded into an F-4N post-war. Transferred to VMFA-323 in 1977, the jet served with the unit until it was lost in a fatal accident on the Leach Lake Range near NAF China Lake, California, on 15 April 1981.

18
F-4J-39-MC BuNo 155894/NK 201 of VF-142, USS *Enterprise* (CVAN-65), 1972-73

Flown by squadron CO Cdr Thomas E Bruyere in 1972-73, this F-4J has a typical CAP ordnance load – as well as the rarely seen underwing tanks. Very occasionally, US Navy F-4s would carry these drop tanks, in addition to the semi-permanent centreline tank, for longer-ranging missions into Laos and Cambodia, where in-flight refuelling was unavailable. As VF-193, the squadron adopted the F-4B in 1963, becoming VF-142 in the process. After four WestPac cruises it transitioned to the F-4J, winning a Battle Efficiency Award primarily for managing improvements in AIM-7 missile effectiveness. In September 1972, on VF-142's seventh combat cruise, it provided support for *Linebacker* operations. This F-4J subsequently served with a series of US Marine Corps units (including VMFA-212 and VMFAT-101) before being transferred to the RAF's No 74 Sqn as F-4J(UK) ZE364, with whom it served from 1984 until 1991. The jet was scrapped in April 1996.

19
F-4J-34-MC BuNo 155740/NK 211 of VF-142, USS *Enterprise* (CVAN-65), 1972-73

Assigned to Lts Farnes White and S P Crall, this F-4J is depicted here loaded with Mk 82 Mod 2 TP 500-lb GP bombs with Mk 15 Snakeye fins, in addition to its air-to-air AIM-9G and AIM-7E-2 weapons. This aircraft later became VF-21's 'CAG bird' in 1980, and also flew with VF-121, surviving as an F-4S until December 1991. It was then converted into a QF-4S and expended. VF-142's colour scheme was retained throughout its seven combat cruises, changing to an all-yellow tail and fuselage stripe for its single Atlantic Fleet deployment with CVW-8 on board *America* in 1974 – the scalloped demarcation line between the undersurface white and gull grey was seen on a number of VF-142 jets. The 'Ghostriders' transitioned to the F-14A in 1975 as part of CVW-6.

20
F-4B-21-MC BuNo 152239/NK 302 of VF-143, USS *Constellation* (CVA-64), late 1969

This bomb-laden F-4J has the names of Cdr Bill Albertson and Lt(jg) J A 'Scotty' McKenzie on its canopies and the AN/APR-25 Shoehorn ECM fit. In January 1969 the squadron commander was Cdr Dave Grosshuesch, but Cdr Albertson took over for the August 1969-May 1970 cruise. After previous service with VF-92 and then with VF-143, the aircraft passed to VF-161 as NL 210, and it was lost on 17 May 1970 with that unit. An engine fire broke out as it was launched from *Coral Sea* on a night strike mission and it dived into the sea seconds later. RIO Lt J Kane, who had been correctly command-ejected first, survived, but no trace of pilot Lt Norman Westwood Jr was ever found.

21
F-4J-34-MC BuNo 155741/NK 110 of VF-143, USS *Enterprise* (CVAN-65), February 1972

Lt Bill Snyder and Lt(jg) Bob Beal put their names on this F-4J for the squadron's sixth wartime cruise, the first on board *Enterprise*. A revised colour scheme using red to replace blue was introduced for two years, and the 'vomiting dog' logo (properly known as a griffin, representing the squadron's previous official name) was moved to a fuselage location. Blue reappeared as the dominant colour

for VF-143's final F-4 deployment (with the Atlantic Fleet) before transition to the F-14A commenced in 1974. VF-143 flew one of the war's final combat missions on 27 January 1973 – the day that the ceasefire was signed – when its CO, Cdr Harley Hall, and RIO Lt Cdr Philip Kientzler were shot down by AAA near Quang Tri. Hall was apparently shot, but Kientzler, with 500 combat missions in his log-book, became the last naval airman to be made a PoW in North Vietnam. Serving with VF-121 following its time with VF-143, BuNo 155741 was upgraded into an F-4S in the late 1970s and then passed on to the US Marine Corps. It was eventually withdrawn from use at MCAS Cherry Point, North Carolina, in July 1994.

22
F-4B-28-MC BuNo 153059/NF 200 of VF-151, USS *Midway* (CVA-41), November 1971

This colourful F-4B served as the CAG aircraft for CVW-5 CO Capt Ralph B Rutherford during VF-151's 1971 WestPac, and it was still the squadron's CAG aircraft in 1972-73, when Capt C E Myers' name was marked on its canopy rail. The pressures of combat activity at sea took a heavy toll on aircraft paintwork, despite frequent hosing down and corrosion control work, and only minor re-touching of the finish was possible aboard ship. The CAG aircraft naturally received plenty of close attention to its appearance, however. By 1972, many of the maintenance stencils that had covered Phantom IIs in the 1960s had been over-painted during maintenance work. Upgraded into an F-4N post-war, BuNo 153059 was sent to MASDC at Davis-Monthan AFB in June 1977 and eventually expended as a QF-4N drone in a missile test on 12 July 1995.

23
F-4N-03-MC BuNo 150634/NF 207 of VF-151, USS *Midway* (CVA-41), September 1973

As the Vietnam War finally wound down in the summer of 1973, re-worked F-4Ns began to reach the carrier force, including this example assigned to Lt 'Apple' Valley and Lt(jg) Dave Sellers. It still had redundant housings for its previous AN/APR-30 ECM system and had not yet received the intake-mounted antennas for the Sanders AN/ALQ-126 DECM system, installed in the mid-1970s. This aircraft served briefly with the USAF, on loan for training purposes as 62-12174, in 1963, and upon its return to the US Navy the jet became a VF-151 MiG killer for Lt Cdr Dan Macintyre and Lt(jg) Allen Johnson on 6 October 1965. BuNo 150634 flew with seven US Navy and US Marine Corps units in total, beginning and ending with VF-151, before entering storage in 1977. It was eventually expended as a target on the Indian Springs bombing range, in Nevada, in June 1983.

24
F-4J-34-MC BuNo 155755/NE 224 of VF-154, USS *Ranger* (CVA-61), May 1971

This squadron received F-4Js in 1968 after two combat tours with B-models Phantom IIs, and it remained with CVW-2 embarked in *Ranger* for four more. BuNo 155755 is armed with five-inch diameter Zuni rockets in LAU-10 four-tube launchers. Powered by Mk 71 Mod 0 motors, these projectiles were formidable as flak-suppression weapons. Assigned to unidentified aircrew that went by the call-signs of 'Dixxy' and 'Selfish', this F-4J was tended by plane captain Perez Wynn. Following subsequent service with VF-121 and VF-92 (it joined the latter unit as an attrition replacement in the spring of 1972 whilst the 'Silver Kites' were still in TF 77 on board *Constellation*), BuNo 155755 was one of the surplus J-models converted for RAF use as F-4J(UK) ZE362. Assigned to No 74 Sqn from 1984 to 1991, the aircraft was scrapped in 1994.

25
F-4J-46-MC BuNo 158357/NE 210 of VF-154, USS *Ranger* (CVA-61), January 1972

Having returned from *Ranger*'s 1970-71 combat cruise, with 123 days 'on the line', this aircraft changed its Modex side-number to NE 110, with new black walkway areas, for the unit's final 1972-73 period in the Gulf of Tonkin. It was later re-numbered as NE 101 and then NE 111. Unlike many F-4s at the time, the jet retained a full set of maintenance stencils. VF-154 sustained no combat losses and only one operational loss with the F-4J, but sister-squadron VF-21 was not so fortunate, losing seven J-models during the same period. This aircraft was destroyed on 12 May 1974 after a mid-air collision with VA-145 KA-6D tanker BuNo 152637 (the latter was also lost) whilst conducting local EastPac training operations off the southern California coast.

26
F-4B-15-MC BuNo 150996/NF 106 of VF-161, USS *Midway* (CVA-41), 1972-73

This aircraft was assigned to Lt Marc Ostertag (who later led F-14-equipped VF-102 and eventually became CO of *Constellation* in the mid-1990s) and Lt(jg) Kenneth Crandall, and it is resplendent in one of the most attractive Phantom II finishes of them all. VF-161 destroyed four VPAF fighters in May 1972 and a fifth (the last US Navy kill) in January 1973. A sixth had been shot down by the unit in July 1972. Ken Crandall was RIO for Lt Mike Rabb in 'Rock River 106', wingman to VF-161's operations officer Lt Cdr 'Mugs' McKeown and his RIO Lt Jack Ensch, for a 23 May 1972 MiGCAP over Kep airfield. In a swirling dogfight with four MiG-17s and two MiG-19s, McKeown and Ensch managed to shoot down two 'Fresco-Cs', one of which was threatening Rabb and Crandall.

27
F-4B-21-MC BuNo 152243/NF 101 of VF-161, USS *Midway* (CVA-41), late 1972

This much-used F-4B, assigned to squadron CO Cdr Wayne 'Deacon' Connell ahead of VF-161's 1972 cruise, completed two tours with the unit and was also operated by VF-21, VF-51 and three US Marine Corps squadrons prior to its retirement in 1982. The 'Chargers' were involved in the conflict from May 1966, shooting down their first MiG-17 on 13 June that year. Post-war, the unit moved to NAF Atsugi, in Japan, with the rest of CVW-5, being assigned to *Midway*, which was homeported at Yokosuka. Both VF-151 and VF-161 were involved in providing fighter cover for the evacuation of Americans from Saigon in 1975. By then, however, F-4Ns had replaced both units' war-weary F-4Bs. BuNo 152243 was also upgraded into an N-model in the mid-1970s, subsequently serving with VF-51 and VMFA-323 until it was struck off charge at NAF China Lake, California, on 17 September 1982.

28
F-4J-41-MC BuNo 157272/NH 100 of VF-213, USS *Kitty Hawk* (CVA-64), 1971-72

Replaced as the unit's 'CAG bird' by BuNo 155882 later in 1972, this F-4J was assigned to Cdr Huntington Hardisty and RIO Lt Wes Voelker. 'Hunt' Hardisty was among the earliest US Navy Phantom II pilots, and he achieved a world low-level speed record of 900 mph at a mean 300 ft altitude in 'Sageburner' F4H-1 BuNo 145307 in 1961. After his time as commander of CVW-11, Hardisty took on increasingly prestigious appointments, retiring as Commander-in-Chief, US Pacific Command in 1991. BuNo 157272 was transferred to VF-121 in 1974 and upgraded into an F-4S two years later. It then served for many years with VMFA-232 until placed in storage with the Aerospace Maintenance and Regeneration Center (AMARC, formerly MASDC) in November 1988 when the unit transitioned to the F/A-18A Hornet.

29
F-4J-40-MC BuNo 157242/NH 102 of VF-213, USS *Kitty Hawk* (CVA-63), May 1972

Assigned to Cdr Reg R Brown (squadron XO) and Lt Cdr Ron J Laib, this F-4J is loaded for a radar bombing mission during the *Linebacker* attacks on North Vietnamese supply networks. Laib was shot down on an 18 June 1972 mission, with MiG killer Lt Cdr Roy Cash as his pilot, when their F-4J was hit by 23 mm AAA during a low-altitude ship attack. Both were recovered by helicopter. NH 102 was transferred to sister-squadron VF-114 in 1974, subsequently flying with VF-121 and VMFA-312 (as an F-4S) until struck off charge in April 1987.

30
F-4J-36-MC BuNo 155852/AJ 201 of VMFA-333, USS *America* (CV-66), December 1972

Just minutes after their success against a MiG-21 on 10 September 1972, Maj Lee Lasseter and Capt John Cummings had to eject from their assigned F-4J BuNo 155526. It was replaced by BuNo 155852, and their names and two MiG kills (initially displayed in diagonal format) were painted on it — only one kill was confirmed. 'Bear' Lasseter became squadron commander in December 1972, taking over from Lt Col John Cochran, who was injured in the 23 December 1972 shoot-down of VMFA-333 aircraft BuNo 153885. The squadron made four F-4J carrier deployments on board *America* and USS *Nimitz* (CVN-68) up to 1977, and eventually transitioned to the F/A-18A in 1987. BuNo 155852 had served with VF-143 and VF-74 prior to joining VMFA-333, and post-war it spent time with VF-121 and VMFA-451. Upgraded into an F-4S in the late 1970s, the aeroplane was placed in storage within AMARC in April 1986.

INDEX

Note: locators in **bold** refer to illustrations and captions.